TWELVE AROUND THE WORLD

Books by Maureen Daly

SEVENTEENTH SUMMER

SMARTER AND SMOOTHER

MY FAVORITE STORIES

THE PERFECT HOSTESS

WHAT'S YOUR P.Q.

TWELVE AROUND THE WORLD

TWELVE

AROUND THE

WORLD

By

MAUREEN DALY

Illustrated by Frank Kramer

DODD, MEAD & COMPANY

NEW YORK, 1957

Library of Congress Catalog Card Number: 57-12034

Printed in the United States of America
by The Cornwall Press, Inc., Cornwall, N. Y.

TO

Megan

my favorite traveler

MEET "TWELVE AROUND THE WORLD"

ARE YOU ALL RICH IN AMERICA? Is every building a sky-scraper? Do your young people really have so much freedom? Are there still gangsters in Chicago and wild Indians in the West? Do you want war, or peace?

Teen-agers everywhere are curious about the United States. Perhaps they admire us, perhaps they distrust us—but they *are* curious and full of questions. And after the first few questions are answered, the subject is changed. They want to talk about themselves. They want to be considered interesting and worth knowing about, too.

That is the reason for this book. The Francine Achs of Paris, the Pepe Gomezes of the Canary Islands and the Brigitte Zahns of West Berlin want your curiosity and interest. They want to tell about themselves.

It took nearly two years and many thousands of miles to meet this "round the world dozen" and write their stories. This book is meant to answer the questions they hope you might want to ask.

CONTENTS

TWELVE AROUND THE WORLD

1

JASMINA NACIRI

Morocco

ONE COOL SUMMER NIGHT, I went to an Arab wedding in the casbah section of Tangier. At ten o'clock, we picked our way through the twisted, narrow little streets, damp and smelling of donkeys and lit only by the dimmest lamp lights. Here and there, the rough cobblestones were brightened by squares of light falling from open doorways or by the glow of hot charcoal *pans* set in front of tiny native restaurants. Over the coals, skewered shiskebabe sizzled and sputtered. Everywhere there was the faint noise of trickling water and the shuffling sound of Arab slippers as passers-by brushed against us at narrow corners.

According to old Arab custom, the wedding celebration was a double-header, with the female friends and relatives meeting at the house of the bride, while the others had their mint tea and festivities at the home of the groom. It was there that the young bride was to be delivered, veiled and in bridal splendor, at about four o'clock in the morning. We were guests of the groom, a tall, very nervous young man, who stood at the entrance of his house with his father, greeting guests in a cordial but shaking voice. His wedding costume was just like his everyday street clothes but new and fresh, a brown and gray striped *djellaba* and a red tasseled fez that lent little color to his pale face. He was not quite twenty years old and his bride was sixteen.

The house, its simple whitewashed walls fronting on a narrow street, was built around a big, square courtyard, two stories high and open to the sky. This courtyard was walled, man-high, with tiles in blue, orange and white and the corners were filled with tall potted plants. At the left, a tile-trimmed doorway arched into a long, narrow sitting room, decorated in Arab style with satin-finished wall hangings in pale pink, lettuce green, yellow and gray, topped with curves and arches of the same fabric. There was no furniture here, except the low, fat, velvet-covered bolsters for sitting—each about five feet long—that lined the sides of the room.

Following the custom, we left our shoes just outside this doorway, setting them carefully beside a dozen pairs of *baboushes,* the sturdy, backless scuff slippers in pastel leather, worn by both men and women. The guests, all men except for me, ran in age from the late teens to two octogenarians,

[2]

brown and wrinkled as walnuts, talking in low, cordial voices and puffing on small-bowled hashish pipes. Each guest wore his immaculate wedding-best *djellaba,* a long-sleeved, ankle-length gown in plain white or brown and black stripes, often put on over a Western-type suit. Several of the older guests wore the distinctive white turban which showed they had made a holy pilgrimage to Mecca. There were no windows in this bright little room and, as newcomers crowded in, the air was soon stiflingly thick with hashish smoke and formality.

Later, with the younger guests, we arranged ourselves cross-legged on bolsters in the courtyard, leaning back against the cool tile walls, to wait for the orchestra to begin playing. Off to one side of the court, in a roofed alcove, a half dozen musicians squatted on heavy straw mats, arranging and tuning their drums, tambourines, flutes and a single violin with the thin metallic tone of a musical saw. Soon the high, singsong Arab music filled the house, sounding out plaintively and insistently for several hours without a break. Little children from the neighborhood, some in tattered rags, crowded in from the street but as new guests arrived, the little ones were shushed back out into the night. The entire celebration was marked by formal behavior and grave, careful courtesy. There were no hasty comings and goings. Each invited guest took a seat, folded his long robes around him and settled down to enjoy himself and the long wait.

At about eleven o'clock, a bustle began. The three younger brothers of the groom started the complicated task of offering refreshments to the fifty or more guests. The kitchen was a curtained-off room on one side of the courtyard and periodically female hands would push supplies through the slit in the curtains and quickly disappear. (Even in small family groups, Arab men and women rarely dine together. Here, women at work in the kitchen would not show themselves before the male guests at all.) First came trays with beaten silver kettles filled with warm water, bowls and hand towels. Each guest held out his hands to have a little water poured over the fingertips, then dried them. The brothers moved briskly about the room, smiling, bowing. Next came a tray with several ornate shakers of jasmine water, passed from hand to hand. The guests shook themselves liberally with the sweet-scented fragrance, sprinkling the scent on hands and wrists, over the head and even down the loose neck of the *djellaba*. Out of the kitchen curtains were shoved deep baskets of wedding bread, big flattish rolls the size of saucers, thin-crusted and smooth as cake and sweetened with milk and honey. With these rolls went mint tea, so sweet and so hot that each glass had to be grasped carefully for drinking, from bottom to rim between thumb and middle finger. The brothers prepared for the main course by bringing out heavy brass trays, rolling them across the room like cartwheels. These trays were arranged, one for every six or seven guests, on sturdy legs just a few inches from the floor, and the boys then set them with bowls of spoons, glasses of water and one giant main dish per tray of *cous cous,* the national dish. This was a wedding *cous cous,* made with the usual fine semolina from the tips of the wheat, like fine brown rice, covering three whole chickens cooked until meltingly tender and decorated with strips of cooked carrots and fat, hot raisins, all served with a peppery sauce.

Guests leaned from their bolsters or squatted around the tray, pulling apart the chicken and eating with three fingers

[4]

of the right hand and either rolling the *cous cous* flour into balls to pop into the mouth or simply using spoons. (Arabs always wash their hands very carefully before eating and then use the right hand only, saving the left to eat foods which one does not like—an insult to the host rarely practiced. In strictest etiquette, it is considered correct to put food into the mouth without even touching the lips.)

The *cous cous* was followed by yellow half-moons of melon and more mint tea. Hands flashed in and out of the kitchen curtain, serving fresh food and collecting the used dishes stacked on a table near the door until the last guest was satisfied. By tradition, the womenfolk of the family or the servants then dine on what food is left. In the background, the orchestra played on and on, with the musicians sometimes singing out high, thin chants that matched the strange cadence of the music.

Once, from the top floor of the house, the tiny cry of an infant echoed down into the courtyard. A few moments later, a plump female figure, wrapped in a long brown garment with a hood and a strip of white cloth covering her face to the eyes, hurried down the stairs, across the courtyard and out the door. No one spoke to her or commented on her presence. A few minutes later, she hurried back up the way she had come, carrying a wine bottle filled with milk and stoppered with a twist of newspaper. In a moment or two the baby's crying faded below the noise of the orchestra and then stopped completely.

Occasionally, from the upper floors, we heard strange sounds—wild, prolonged howls and isolated, lingering hoots that had no particular note of gaiety or celebration. But at each startling shriek, the guests just smiled. I asked a man

[5]

who spoke Spanish what it meant and he said, "Oh, the women servants upstairs are doing that to tease the groom. They keep it up all night—even after the bride arrives." It reminded me of the old "charivari" custom in some parts of the United States, when neighborhood children sneak up late at night to serenade newlyweds with horns and pots and pans. Looking up, I could see the figures of the servant women leaning over the top floor railing, hooded and veiled, like Hallowe'en figures in the shadowy light.

This was a middle-class household (the father was a small local merchant, the groom his oldest son) but the hospitality was meticulous and lavish. The head of the house had negotiated this marriage and now wanted to show the relatives of the bride that he was not only prosperous but generous. It is against the Moslem religious laws to drink alcoholic beverages but most of the guests treated the mint tea like free champagne and sipped glass after glass through the night. The air was thick with the sweet steam of the tea, the fragrance of jasmine and the clinging mist of hashish smoke. But the entire celebration pointed to the zero hour of four o'clock when the groom and some of his family would go to fetch the bride.

A small wooden litter, or *almiryah,* stood just outside the front doorway all evening. It was a simple litter, not more than four feet high and coming to a cone-shape on top, with a carved wooden frame painted green and gilt, and side curtains of dull red cloth. This litter was made to be carried by four sturdy men or lashed to the back of a little donkey. Rented just for the evening, its touches of gilt and battered trimmings looked both sadly feminine and non-festive, like something left over from a bankrupt carnival.

[6]

At the bride's house, the young girl would at this moment be sitting in ceremonious splendor, while female friends and relatives crowded around to admire and offer best wishes. Next would come the feast and drinking of mint tea. During this part of the wedding ceremony, the bride is expected by tradition not to laugh, smile or show pleasure but to keep her eyes decorously cast floorward as a sign of purity and modesty.

At four o'clock, after she had been carried to her husband's house in the litter, preceded through the dark little streets by musicians and well-wishers carrying candles, the young bride would be met by one servant. This servant would lift her from the litter, carrying her carefully to her husband's chamber, since her feet must not touch the ground in this part of the ceremony. Later, when he has finished celebrating with his men friends, the husband will join his new wife —and see her face unveiled for the first time. Then follows a nuptial feast, just for the bride and groom, perhaps the last meal she will ever eat with him, since usually the females of a family dine apart.

After her wedding day, the young bride begins life with the groom's family (until the day they may have their own home), rarely leaving the house and never going on the street unless carefully veiled. In strictly orthodox families, no male except the husband—and children—is ever allowed to see the wife's face uncovered.

It was two o'clock before we left the wedding party, heads ringing with music, eyes heavy with the steamy atmosphere and the hot tea. The young bridegroom saw us to the street, leaning for a moment against the doorjam, as if he felt faint. He shook my hand again and again, repeating lavish thanks

[7]

for the box of chocolates we had brought as a wedding present. Nervously, he was waiting out the last hours, apprehensive to learn what fate—and the arrangements of two sets of parents—had picked as his wife. He behaved at this last moment very much as if he would have liked to forget the whole thing and come out with us into the dark, impersonal streets. However, I heard later that he turned up at his favorite cafe for coffee at eight sharp the next morning, happy and eager to tell the boys that his luck had been very good indeed.

Two days after that wedding, I met Jasmina Naciri. She was the first teen-aged Arab girl I had found who was willing to talk to me and let me write her story. We sat in the third floor apartment of a friend, in the downtown section of Tangier, with the week-end noises of the traffic and crowds floating up from the streets of that cosmopolitan coastal city. Jasmina's parents had forbidden her to see me, so she had come in secret because she felt that this interview was so very important to carry out her dreams for the women of Morocco.

Her voice was soft and shy, yet she spoke determinedly, in good, schoolgirl English. "I'm sorry I can only see you for an hour today," she said apologetically, "and perhaps for an hour tomorrow. But I think you will understand when I tell you more about our customs. My parents did not want me to come at all today. They said that to talk about one's self in such a public way is just not right for a *nice* Arab girl."

Jasmina is an Arab by birth and a Moslem by religion and according to strict custom, should have been wearing the female version of a *djellaba,* the ankle-length kimonalike garment, with long sleeves and a loose hood, usually white for women but sometimes worn in navy pin-stripe serge by the fashion-conscious females of Tangier. And like orthodox Moslem women, her features should have been covered with a piece of veiling the size of a large tea napkin, knotted in the back and covering the face right up to her expressive green eyes. (It is not usual for Moslem women to wear make-up but occasionally, in Tangier and the large cities, a pair of heavily mascaraed eyes flashes above the face veil and high-heeled French shoes click along under the flapping *djellaba*). But Jasmina sat facing me like a serious, well-groomed American high school student, all dressed up for Sunday.

Her dress was green silk jersey, printed with brown and white roses and she wore white sandals, a strand of pearls and little pearl earrings. Only her hair style seemed old-fashioned: long, light brown hair tied back with a velvet ribbon, low on the neck, like a loose pony tail. Most Arabs are light-skinned, as is Jasmina, and her delicate coloring, without lipstick, made her seem younger than eighteen. In all of Tangier (there are about 160,000 people here, one-third of whom are Moslems), Jasmina is one of only about a dozen Arab girls who has decided to defy the customs of centuries and dress as she pleases. Down in the city of Rabat, capital of Morocco, lovely twenty-four-year-old Princess Lalla, oldest daughter of Sultan Ben Youssef, has also put aside the veil, thus giving courage to other young Moslems to break tradition.

"I don't like to fool my parents as I am doing today," Jasmina explained hastily, "because they *do* try to understand

[9]

me and they *have* given me freedom in so many things. But I wanted to talk to you. I have made up my mind that it will be my life's work to learn how to make life for women here more "modern"—and then write about it so other Moroccans may learn. Let me tell you something about what life is like for an Arab girl here . . ."

And this is the beginning of her story: "One day when I was twelve years old, I decided to keep a diary. And I have written in it every day since. My first words in that diary were, *'Today I am angry. I cannot go out. I want to be free!'*

"I remember that day very clearly. We were living then in the casbah. (The casbah is the ancient, walled section of the city of Tangier, the same section to which I had gone for the wedding party. Many gleaming modern apartment buildings have now sprung up outside those walls, but these are chiefly the homes of European residents of Tangier. The Jews and the Arabs, the older residents of the city, are mostly crowded into the casbah section.)

"A younger girl friend of mine was having a birthday party in her home and I was invited. And I wanted to go very much. Now it is the Moslem custom (and both of my parents are devoted Moslems) that as soon as a girl reaches maturity and is considered a woman, she begins to wear the long gown, instead of children's dresses, and is always veiled, except in her own home. Once she wears the veil, she is expected to stay in the house more, out of sight. It happened that, even though I was already twelve years old, my parents had not yet insisted that I begin to wear a veil. They thought I was pretty and just didn't want me to cover my face. I am an only child and they rather spoil me. (In Morocco, male

[10]

children are valued more highly than females. In the old days, female children were sometimes strangled at birth and even today it is customary to offer commiserations rather than congratulations on the birth of a daughter. But human love is often stronger than custom and Jasmina, like many other Arab daughters, is a much-loved girl.)

"But on the day of that birthday party my mother said to me for the first time, 'Jasmina, you cannot go out today. It is not safe for you nor good for your reputation to be seen on the streets so often. From now on, you must stay home with us. I want people to think of you as a nice girl.'

"I stayed home that day and began my diary. Even though I couldn't go to the birthday party, I knew I still had a better life than some of my friends. The day an Arab girl puts on the veil is like the beginning of a prison sentence. After that, she goes almost nowhere, except perhaps to a movie suitable for children. (In fact, in Tangier there is a law forbidding Moslem women to go to movies at all; and when the wives of the wealthy men go for afternoon drives, they go heavily veiled, often in cars with curtained windows.) Perhaps she can go to the beach—but never in a bathing suit, as she might as a child. Now she must just sit in the sand or go wading, veiled right up to the eyes. It is sometimes very hot here in the summertime. (Exactly as Jasmina described them, I have seen many Moslem women on the beaches on hot summer days, veiled to the eyes, but laughing nevertheless and having a wonderful time as they stood at the water's edge, letting the waves splash over their bare feet.)

"Most girls just stay at home," Jasmina went on, "helping to run the house, tending the younger children or doing fine embroidery work, hour after hour. That is why we have so

[11]

many beautiful pillows, cloths and bedspreads covered with embroidery—young girls have so much time.

"Until she marries, an Arab girl is completely under the control of her parents. After marriage, she is under the control of her husband. Most Arab men are hot-blooded and jealous. They love strongly and they like their wives in their homes for themselves alone. But most girls are willing to marry men they have never seen, just to have some change in life, a chance to get away from home.

"The day of that birthday party I thought and thought and I knew I wanted my life to be different. I wanted three things: never to wear a veil, to get an education and to choose the man I wanted to marry. And I wanted to be his only wife. (According to Moslem custom, a man may marry up to four wives, as long as all are treated equally, but the current high cost of living usually limits a household to one or two wives. A wealthy Moroccan may have all four wives, plus a harem of women of his choice, all living harmoniously under one roof. Sultan Mohammed Ben Youssef has two wives and once had forty concubines. His second wife, a beautiful ex-servant girl, was given to him as a gift some years ago by the Pasha of Marrakesh.)

"I had my first wish when my parents did not insist on the veil," explained Jasmina, "but I had to *beg* for my second wish—an education. We are poor people—my father is a taxi driver here in Tangier—and many poor people do not send their children to school at all. Certainly most girls leave school here when they are twelve. (Less than 10 per cent of all school-aged Moroccan children attend school.) But I begged my parents to let me go to one of the big public schools in town—the same as your high schools, I think. So until I was graduated last year, I studied with Arab, French, English and Spanish students."

The problem of education in Morocco is very complex. Since Morocco has been a free country only since March, 1956, and it was for many years before that time under the protectorates of France and Spain, those two countries were responsible for building schools. *Some* schools were built but education for the native Moroccans was not always encouraged and now nearly ninety per cent of all Moroccans can neither read nor write. However, by most, this is not considered a disgrace. One of the last Sultans, Mohammed Ben Moulay Arafa, was a wealthy and powerful man who could neither read nor write. For such needs, it was always possible to hire an educated servant. Yet, I remember that in several of the isolated desert towns in the south of Morocco, the great brown walls were plastered with posters showing current Sultan Ben Youssef, arms outstretched, looming over a schoolhouse into which were pouring Moroccans of all ages. These posters would indicate that Moroccans today would value more education very much.

Many little Moslem boys between the ages of three and seven do go to a "Koran school." The book of the Koran—the written word of God or Allah, as revealed to Mohammed, his Chief Prophet—is to the Islamic (or Moslem) religion what the Bible is to the Christian faith. I remember passing a Koran school on one of the casbah streets in Tangier one morning. It was a single room, without windows but open to the street, and little boys sat on the floor, cross-legged and barefooted, reciting in singsong after the teacher the words of the Koran. The teacher also squatted on the floor, leaning so the light from the doorway fell across the parchment in

[13]

his hand. These little Arab boys might never learn to read and write but, at least, they would spend two to four years memorizing the tenets of their religion.

Other young Arabs may get their "schooling" as apprentices, either in state-run schools for learning trades and crafts or as on-the-job workers. Boys of no more than eight work long hours in the little shops of tailors, wood carvers and leather workers. In Casablanca, I visited a rug factory, a large, two-story, cement garage, where little girls from six years to twelve worked nine hours a day, hand-weaving huge rugs hanging on looms from the ceiling. Among the group were several young mothers, their infants in baskets by their sides. The girls sat on narrow, backless benches, weaving, knotting and cutting on rugs that took as long as five months to make. And a female supervisor walked among the benches, a switch in her hand, to hurry on any little fingers that worked too slowly.

"I go to a private school in the morning now," Jasmina explained about herself. "It is a school run by an English woman for students between eighteen and twenty who want to study languages or literature. I pay about nine dollars a month to go to this school and, right now, I'm studying English and French poetry. In fact," she said with a laugh, "I put something in my diary last night about my studies. I wrote that I like the plays of Oscar Wilde very much—and I will always judge a writer by his work, not by his private life!"

"A few years ago, we moved out of the casbah into an apartment in the medina (the newer section of town). When I'm not at school or at work, I spend most of my time there, just reading and studying.

[14]

"In the afternoon, I have a job as a secretary with the city government of Tangier," she said proudly. "I learned to type in school and I'm the only Arab girl employed by the city. My parents were very kind about this, too. It's completely against tradition for an Arab girl to work outside the house. I earn about three thousand pesetas (around seventy-five dollars) a month and give it all to my father. Then he gives me back the money I need for school and clothes. The rest he is saving for his life's dream—to build a little villa of his own in the country before he dies.

"Even though I have freedom to work and study," said Jasmina a little sadly, "I have little freedom in other things. I am never allowed to go to movies except with my teacher. Sometimes she takes me to the Cine Club, a club where amateur photographers show their films. About once a week I go to the library. Other times, I am at home with my parents. But I read and study for nearly three hours at night. So I am busy."

Jasmina glanced at her wristwatch and said shyly, "My hour is almost up. Can I tell you the rest tomorrow?" The next day was Sunday, a religious holiday in the Christian sections of Tangier, but just another weekday in the Arab-Moslem world. We agreed to meet at eleven o'clock, in a public garden.

"But tomorrow I must hurry, too," warned Jasmina. "My father drives all round the city in his taxi and I'm afraid he might see me talking to you." Then she hurried away.

*   *   *

With nearly twenty-four hours before I could see Jasmina again, I had an excellent chance to wander through her city.

[15]

Tangier is a crowded, colorful seaside town on one of the northernmost tips of Africa. All of Morocco has an area little larger than California, with a population of about 10,000,-000, and Tangier is the glamour city of the north. For thirty years—and until just recently—Tangier was an "international zone," physically a part of Morocco but governed by a committee made up of representatives of the United States, Belgium, France, Great Britain, Holland, Italy, Portugal and Spain.

Viewed from the sea, Tangier is a postcard town, a brilliant and precise picture of busy docks and modern apartment buildings, gleaming white against the low, gray mountains and blue sky. In good weather, the gardens are fragrant with jasmine and bright with bougainvillea; tall palm trees stretch above garden walls and the miles of beach glisten in the sun. The winter months are chill, with wind and driving rain. The newer section of the city is an elegant potpourri of expensive restaurants, international banks, chic shops with clothes from Paris and broad, traffic-crowded boulevards. Most streets have French names but every street sign is printed in three languages—French, Spanish and Arabic—and many people in Tangier can speak all three.

In stark contrast to the newer part of the city is the native quarter—the crumbling, ancient casbah, crowded with tiny streets and narrow houses; its thick walls, once used as protection against enemies, still standing. The casbah has been in existence for hundreds of years, while the newer sections of the city have sprung up chiefly in the last three decades. In Tangier, there are great contrasts between the European and Moorish ways of life and between the rich and poor—the rich Arabs as well as the rich Europeans. The center streets

[16]

hum with expensive cars, while in the shadows of every wall, a shabby beggar huddles, pleading for alms in the name of Allah. The homes of the wealthy Arabs are palatial, staffed with dozens of servants; the Sultan of all Morocco is paid nearly a million dollars a year—and the average Moroccan laborer earns twenty-six cents an hour.

Since Jasmina's first home had been the casbah, I decided to try to find it. First I had to walk through the Grand Socco, the giant, sprawling outdoor market, about four square blocks in size, right outside one of the casbah gates. Here the stalls and counters are set up in the streets each market day, then stripped clean and emptied by nightfall. Friday is the Moslem holy day, a day of rest from business, but on Saturday shops are wide open and the market place had the noisy, pushing atmosphere of a street brawl. Everything was color, confusion, sound and movement. People in this area and climate shop for food by the day, sometimes by the meal, and the market is crowded from dawn till dusk, and in the dusk oil lamps light the booths till night falls.

Heaps of figs, grapes, melons and dates lay spread on open tables, a sweet mixture of color and fragrance; other stalls were piled with tomatoes, red and green peppers, curled squash and garlic bulbs, while big purple onions, with their stems braided together in ropey bunches, hung like a fringe from great baskets. Here and there, merchants without stall space simply squatted on the sidewalk and spread their goods in a neat circle around them. Occasionally, an old man sat propped against a wall, his complete stock for the day—two or three bright-eyed little chickens with tied legs—on the ground before him. Rickety stalls were burdened with conglomerate piles of glassware, plastic combs, shoelaces, silk

[17]

scarves, and dark glasses; buckets of fresh flowers lined the curbstone, adding a spicy fragrance. Bearded, turbaned snake-charmers sang and jumped in cleared spaces; little donkeys picked their way over the pavement, bulging saddle-bags nudging a wider path through the crowd. Over everything hung the tangy smell of fresh mint, used in great quantities for mint tea, lying cool and bright green in flat straw baskets. One of the strangest sights was the letter writers—men crouched on curbstones, with notepaper, ink and dip pen, waiting to act as secretary for a few cents to any illiterate who had a message to send.

The goods of the great market fell into sections—the walled courtyard for twigs and charcoal at one end, the straw goods of baskets, rugs and donkey panniers at another, and the open-fronted stalls of fluttering used clothing, blue jeans to limp satins, lining the streets over near the mosque. The clamor, the sounds of animal and human voices, rose and fell over the market like the rhythmic crash of rough seas.

At the few simple sidewalk cafes, roughly dressed farmers and city Arabs in impeccable white wool *djellabas* sipped at mint tea or bottled orange pop. But no women stopped to rest there: the Arab woman's place is in the home and she usually seems to be rushing to get there. I watched the city housewives and servants out shopping, burdened with baskets of the day's food, usually leading a child or two by the hand, always veiled and swathed like a walking mummy, hustling and pushing through the crowds.

The country housewife, in town to sell her basket of fruit, chickens or load of firewood, is often unveiled and her clothe are distinctly those of a Berber woman from the hills. Her manner, too, is more leisurely; the walk over the dusty

[18]

roads is a long one and she will probably spend all day in town before trudging home in the dusk. Though the people of Morocco are generally known as Moors or Moroccans, they are either Berbers or Arabs. To make the distinction as simple as possible, the Berbers are the people who originally inhabited Morocco, centuries ago, before the Arabs invaded the country from Arabia. But both groups practice the Moslem religion. Out of all Moroccan natives, there are three Berbers to every Arab. The Berbers prefer to live in the mountains and farm country, while most Arabs choose the cities—hence the Arabs seem the more conspicuous and numerous people.

On market day in Tangier, the Berber women show up in their hill-country best. This is a complicated costume of several parts. Usually there is a skirt of heavy red and white striped material, pulled tightly over a roll of hip padding that stands out like an innertube (very helpful for carrying baskets), and a heavy white blouse with long sleeves and high neck, covered shawl-wise around the shoulders with more red and white striped goods or a cloth of bright yellow. Over the head goes a full white scarf that is drawn under the chin and tucked loosely into the neck of the blouse. On top of that is balanced a coarse, cartwheel straw hat, decked with furry red pompoms and with a brim so wide and heavy that it is supported by four blue plush strings attached to the crown. (A Berber belle may add small mirrors around the crown of the hat, to glint and shine in the sun.) With all this, big silver loop earrings are worn, and a bracelet or two, plus the distinctive "Berber beauty spots," a series of little blue dots tattooed either up the forehead between the eyes or on the chin, from the lower lip down. Most of the women are barefoot, their feet coarsened and thickened by the city pavements and the rough, country roads. The Berbers are a stocky, hard working group, light-skinned and often blue-eyed, but their faces—though usually lit with good humor—show the marks of harsh weather, strong sun and wet winter winds and a hard life in the hills. Next to them, the Arab city women, taller and often more slim, with face veils tipped in fine crochet work, and in scuff slippers of pale green or blue, look contrastingly elegant and feminine.

After viewing the market place, I wandered through the gate into the casbah and, though I never found the house in which Jasmina had lived, I saw the teeming, crowded life of the area. Little boys, often ragged and dirty, swarmed over the sidewalks at play, women loitered around the street fountains to gossip while filling clay jugs, and in the tiny shops, dark and stuffy, the dignified Arab merchants sipped tea and bargained with customers. The rows of joined houses, whitewashed, with bits of iron balcony, looked shabby from the dirty, twisting streets, but glimpses through open doorways showed cool inside courtyards, bright with flowers and patches of sun. Much of Morocco is dry country (even in busy Tangier the public water supply is shut off each day from two in the afternoon till six the following morning). The Arabs, with century-old memories of thirst, love water and the sound of water and every courtyard has a tiny, tinkling fountain. The casbah was colorful and picturesque but primitive, like a look into life a hundred years past.

Later in the day, I took a taxi out to the apartment building on the Rue Guadalaviar where Jasmina now lives. Because of her concern about her parents, I asked the cab driver to go right past. Her home is well outside Tangier, in a small, three-story white stucco building on a rutted, rundown street that never quite lived up to the real estate agent's dream. A few other apartment buildings stand nearby, also small and shabby, isolated in this disconnected area, as if they were waiting for the rest of the city to grow out to meet them. No colorful courtyards here, no hidden gardens and tinkling fountains. As I passed Jasmina's building, an Arab woman hurried out, adjusting her veil close to her eyes, and scurried off down the street with a market basket.

On the map, Tangier is just the usual "city dot," comparing in size to the whole of Morocco as Sacramento might to the entire state of California. But its sophistication and modernness is very different from most of the sprawling brown plains and rugged mountain areas of the rest of the country.

Along many main roads, for instance, are scattered Berber farm villages, sometimes only a cluster of ten or fifteen round, windowless mud huts, with peaked, cone-shaped straw roofs. Usually these villages are walled around by hedges of paddle cactus and the pointed roof tops are crowned with storks' nests. These big black and white birds spot the Moroccan landscape like a trademark. Much of the work of the fields is done by hand, women and children laboring from dawn till dark, while the men use handplows, drawn by a donkey and camel team, to scratch the earth. These craggy beige camels, common in the countryside, are also used for transportation, as beasts of burden, swaying and bending under loads strapped across their humps, and for turning the windlass that draws water from the community wells. In winter, these barren villages are rain-drenched and

[21]

slick with mud; in summer, they bake under the fierce sun.

Though many Frenchmen and occasional Arabs have built modern, producing farms, most of the farming and country living methods here are as primitive as they were in Biblical times. The country people are highly superstitious and many of the women wear hand of Fatima "good luck pieces," made of silver and as big as dinner plates, hanging around the neck to ward off evil. Little boys and girls have their heads shaved, leaving only a long tuft of hair on one side, or a series of small, unshaven circles, popping out here and there on the skull. (I was told that the idea behind the head shaving is this: if the child is made unattractive enough, Allah—or God—will not be so eager to snatch the little one off to heaven). Even the farming is touched with superstition —or ritual—and before each spring plowing, a Berber farmer will ceremoniously break bread over the handle of his plow, with all the family present, to bring fertility to the soil and the new crop.

Curiously, these primitive villages often lie only a few yards from modern, well-kept highways and while many parts of the country are linked by busy airlines, the bearded, turbaned, djellabed Moroccan jogging side-saddle on his little donkey is still the most typical sight. Morocco has made giant strides toward twentieth-century progress—but too many people and places have been left behind. Still, many prefer it that way.

When the French first came to Morocco, about 125 years ago, it was an isolated, backward country, with pirates still preying out from the coast. But it was a valuable land— rich in beauty, potential ports and, most important, in unmined minerals. Recently, on March 2, 1956, after forty-three years of French rule and several years of brutal, bloody fighting, the country was granted its freedom. Now the biggest buildings and industry are still owned by the French, as they were built by French planning and capital. Huge modern hotels, with luxury accommodations and swimming pools, line the Atlantic coast; giant super-modern structures, planned as apartments, theaters and stores, stand unfinished. In physical fear—and because they didn't want to lose money on bad investments—many French companies simply stopped building and developing. In many ways, Morocco's new freedom has made Moroccan life more difficult. Baffled young Arabs are free—and out of work.

The situation is made worse by the fact that there simply are not enough educated Moroccans to fill the jobs left by the "enemy." When the country became independent, there were—among the 9,000,000 Moslems—only one polytechnician, one doctor of law, five graduate professors, three public works engineers, eighteen lawyers, twenty agricultural engineers, twenty-one medical doctors, forty-two professors of Arabic and less than one hundred university graduates. Hardly enough trained people to govern and run an entire country!

Compared to the rural life, the small town life is often only a little less backward. After driving through miles of flat, arid land, covered with scrub cactus and circled with buzzards, we came one day to the southern town of Tiznit. Outside the high, brown clay walls, a weathered stone sign-post pointed south across the Sahara to the famous trading post of Timbuktu. Inside the town, rough cobbled streets wandered between close-packed houses of clay and stone. Women drew their face veils up to their eyes and turned

[23]

their heads as we passed. The shops and market stalls were crowded but simple, while, above everything, swaying high, were the slim, graceful date palms. We climbed to the rough tower of the mosque and looked out over the town with its endless rows of flat roofs and squared walls, so monotonous and so precise that Tiznit looked like a giant house of cards, built by a whimsical child, using cards made of flat brown mud. The entire town seemed to shimmer and move in the relentless July sun. It appeared not much changed from the days of decades ago when Tiznit was an oasis stop for the weary camel caravans from Timbuktu.

Equally colorful and remote was the town of Chauen, high in mountains of the north. Hundreds and hundreds of years old, no Christian had set foot in Chauen until the 1920's. It stands still, like a small sized casbah, but miles from any other village, without telephone, running water, movie theaters or hospitals—without any of the modern touches that might mark it as part of the twentieth century. It is a jumble of houses—some a chalky, brilliant blue—steep little street fountains and the all-over, lingering stench of bad sanitation—a village of hand-looms, potters' wheels and twig fires.

This difference in degrees of civilization within one country is one reason for the fiery unrest and drive in present day Morocco. For every Jasmina, with a chance and desire for education, there are thousands and thousands of teen-aged boys and girls whose whole world is rimmed by the isolation of primitive life—either high mountains or desolate plains.

(Right now, many Moroccans are extremely hostile to all outsiders; in several areas we were warned bluntly to "get out." However, since the United States has several large military airbases in Morocco and since our government has promised a large sum in economic aid, Americans are—on the whole—quite popular. But I would like to mention one amusing episode of warmth and friendship that had nothing to do with money or politics. In Chauen, in a tiny back-street stall, I saw a long, thick red wool cord, knotted in several places and ending with a bright decorative fringe. I knew it was to wear but didn't know how. I must have seemed puzzled, for a young Berber woman, burdened with baskets, stepped over and took it from my hand. Then she slipped the cord over her shoulders and down around her hips, gesturing and pantomiming to show that it was meant to help carry bundles on the back. With a big, girlish grin she stepped back, marching and pivoting, to model it for me. Her tanned, wind-beaten face was wrinkled with smiles. And neither of us could exchange an understandable word.)

Jasmina and I met in the garden promptly at eleven o'clock on Sunday morning. She had "dressed up" for our meeting and looked very teen-aged and pretty in a dress of soft pink printed rayon.

"This is one of my grown-up dresses." She laughed. "Even though I don't wear Moorish clothes, my mother likes me to dress in childish things, mostly sheer nylon dresses with high necks, full skirts and little puffed sleeves."

We found a bench to sit on and Jasmina began to talk. "Yesterday I told you something about my home life and studies. Today I will tell you something else." Her cheeks suddenly became pink with shyness and excitement. "In a few weeks, a man is going to come to my parents to ask to marry me.

"As you know, it is still a custom in most of Morocco for a girl to marry someone she does not meet until after the wedding. But young people with modern ideas don't like that.

"About six weeks ago, a married girl friend of mine came up from Casablanca to visit her parents. I went to see her and met her husband—and his brother who was with them. The brother was very kind and talked to me a little but I was too shy to answer. Later, my friend wrote that this man said he wanted to marry me."

Was she surprised? "I knew he was very kind and, even though I liked him, I didn't know he liked me. At least I never thought he was thinking of marriage."

And what is he like? "He is older than I, about twenty-eight, short, with a good face—and, most of all, he seems intelligent and has humor. Since I saw him first, my girl friend has written all about him. He and his family are in the textile business and have stores in Casablanca and Marrakesh. He is well educated and has a summer home of his own, with a swimming pool, in Marrakesh. (Marrakesh, the second largest city in Morocco, with a population of nearly a quarter of a million, is one of the loveliest cities of the world. With the snow-capped Atlas mountains ringing it on one side, its center a bedlam of flowering gardens and fountains and its buildings made from the pinkish-red clay of the area, Marrakesh looks like a city eternally touched by sunrise.)

What did she think would happen now? "A few days ago, his sister—an older married sister—came to Tangier and

[26]

called on my mother. She talked about her brother and said that he would like to marry me. My parents have now given him permission to call at our home. In a few weeks, he is coming here to visit us and talk to me."

Did she think she would marry him? "I don't know. I think that eighteen is too young to marry but my mother wants me to. She says, if I have a husband, I will settle down!" Jasmina laughed. "When I marry, my life will just be starting! I won't settle down. You see, this young man is very wealthy and he does not mind that we are poor people. He told my girl friend that he liked me, not only for my manner but because I had taken off the veil and because I had a job. He said he wanted a modern wife, someone with an education who could travel with him and someone who would be pretty and smiling when he came home from his shop. And I want to be a modern wife, too. So if he understands me and the kind of life I want to lead, I think we love each other.

"But I must wait till he calls on my parents. Then—if I feel I can love him—we can become engaged for a year. According to our customs, he would send me engagement gifts, from himself and his family. Usually rolls of fine silk, perfumes and perhaps some jewelry. We can visit each other, always with our parents, of course, and get to know each other until it is time to be married."

Did she think she would make a good wife? "I will try very hard. I don't know much about cooking or housekeeping because we always had a maid. And since I am an only daughter, my mother treats me like a princess. But two years ago I bought a French cookbook. I have studied how to make pastries, roast meat and special sauces. And I have

[27]

watched my mother run the house. Also, he told my girl friend that he likes music, so I think I'll begin to study the piano. And for the year of our engagement, I'll keep at my job and studies. At school, we are planning a production of *Cyrano de Bergerac,* and I will be Roxanne—I wouldn't want to miss that. When we are married, perhaps my husband and I will read together. And I will try to write. . . ."

If she marries, will it be in the Moslem faith? "Yes, yes, yes," she answered quickly. "I will always have my religion. I am interested in the faiths of other people and countries but I will always be a Moslem. I never keep the Fast of Ramadan but my parents do and my father prays five times a day. I think it is a good thing to have a strong religion."

The Moslem holy book, the Koran states, "The month of Ramadan is that in which the Koran was sent down." Ramadan is the ninth month of the Moslem year and Mohammed, the great prophet of the Moslem religion, is believed to have received the first of his revelations for the Koran from God on the Night of Power—the 27th day of Ramadan. Mohammed ordained an entire month of fast days, with no taking of food from dawn to dark, as well as other penances. "Eat and drink until so much of the dawn appears that a white thread may be distinguished from a black, then keep the fast completely until night." Except for young people, or those very old or sick, most Moslems strictly observe the Fast of Ramadan. But just as Jasmina's parents felt she should not be obliged to wear the veil, they were not strict about her fasting.

The practice of "prayers five times a day" is also an important part of the Moslem faith. These prayers must be said, wherever one may be, facing the city of Mecca, Mohammed's birthplace in Arabia. Most Moslems pray at home or at the mosque but it is not unusual to see, in some quiet corner off a busy street, a devout Moslem kneeling in prayer, his forehead touched to the ground.

The first prayer of the day is said at the earliest sign of daylight when the "prayer call" is sung out by the *Muezzin* (holy man) from the minarets—tall, slim towers with an open platform at the top which dot every Moslem town. In noisy sections of town, where the call from the minaret might not be heard above the sounds of the city, a little white flag is run up at prayer time. On Friday, it is imperative for faithful Moslems to go to prayer at the mosque, a building strictly forbidden to all "unbelievers" or non-Moslems.

To understand Jasmina and her people, it is necessary to understand the strength and breadth of the Moslem faith. It is a religion which began in the seventh century and which is now believed in by *one-seventh* of all the people on earth. It is especially strong in Morocco, Egypt, Saudi Arabia, India and Indochina, with several million Moslems in Russia.

I noticed Jasmina glancing nervously at her watch and realized our hour was almost at an end. But I had one more request. I wanted to take her picture. I knew, however, that I might run into another religious "don't" because the Koran expressly forbids "the making of images" and many Moslems feel posing for pictures is therefore forbidden. In the streets and market places, many Moroccans become either frightened or very angry at the sight of a tourist camera. In one remote corner of the casbah, a half-dozen aged, crippled beggars struggled painfully to their feet and limped off when they saw me approaching with a camera slung around my

[29]

neck. But Jasmina answered, "Certainly. I don't believe our religion means no photographs."

When I had finished taking her picture, she said seriously, "I mean it when I say I want to see the world and know more about other people. I love my country but we are changing and we have a lot to learn. We need a chance—especially the young people. Would you tell me where you live in New York because I think I will be there some day. Then you can show me something of American life." I scribbled my address on a slip of paper and, after a few last words, she hurried away, looking at her watch as she left the park. She soon disappeared in the crowd streaming to and from the great market place. Back on Rue Guadalaviar, a worried mother was probably already looking out the windows of the small white apartment building, wondering why Jasmina was out on the streets so long.

2

LUIS HERNANDEZ

Spain

LUIS HERNANDEZ LIVES in Malaga, Spain. This southern
port city which jams 300,000 people along its broad,
newer avenues and crooked, ancient streets is over 2000 years
old. Luis Hernandez is just sixteen.

In his part of town, the old streets twist and bend till the
tiny, overhanging balconies, burdened with flowerpots, seem

to touch in mid-air. It is noisy and crowded, filled with people in every daylight hour and even until late at night. Rickety candy stands, bright with cellophane and cheap plastic toys, lean against the curbs. In the doorways, old women in faded, well-patched black sit sewing and chatting and dozens of cats sun themselves along the windowsills. The movement, the crowds and the children playing and shouting over the rough cobblestones give the neighborhood a bustling, carnival air every day of the week. Luis' home is on Huerto de Monjaz, a poor street in a back section of town, apartment number ten, three flights up and the last door on the left.

Through an inside, open-air courtyard, painted a bright, chalky blue and climbing with geraniums, up two flights of blue stairs, scrubbed clean but still smelling strongly of cats, along a narrow passageway open to the courtyard and to the sky and into the back of the building is Luis' home. A five-room apartment for five people with water and light included rented at only $4.40 a month. The rooms are so small that a sewing machine, covered with a brightly embroidered cloth, and four straight, cane-seated chairs crowd the front parlor, while in the dining room, Luis' aunt, who has cared for the family since his mother died six years ago, has to crowd and push to pass between the single china cabinet and the square, heavy table that sits in the middle of the room.

But this home, a typical apartment for a Spanish working man, is unimportant to Luis. Here he is restless, impatient and often bad-tempered. His aunt putters about the house, sewing and cleaning, in a blue and white dotted dress so old and threadbare that the white dots are falling out. With her —and with his strict father—he is well-mannered and quiet.

[32]

But with his brother and sisters he is different. The older sister is married and lives away from home but his younger sister, a handsome, dark-haired girl of twenty-eight, is still at home and with her he bickers constantly, calling her crossly "my terrible stepmother." To his only brother, a lanky twenty-one-year-old with whom he shares a bedroom, he barely speaks.

"My brother is interested in nothing but his girl friend," Luis says bitterly. "We have nothing to talk about." Luis is happier, more confident, when he is away from home, when he is swimming at one of the Mediterranean beaches, walking with his girl in the palm and orange groves of the city park or—best of all—sitting alone in the movies, dreaming about the sixteen-year-old he would rather be.

Luis was born here in Malaga just two years after the fierce Spanish Civil War ended. For most of his life, shyness and lack of money kept him locked in the narrow, crowded streets around his home. Until six months ago he had never been outside the city limits. Then, one rainy winter day, he took a twelve-cent bus ride—crowded in with shoppers, tourists and ragged native gypsies with baskets of plastic combs and fans to sell—to the fishing village of Torremolinos, seven miles away. Luis makes the same trip two or three times a week, still on the same old bus, but he has not yet worked up courage to go farther along the coast or up into the heart of Spain. And yet he dreams and firmly believes that by the time he is twenty-one, he will have made a trip to New York.

Except for his out-sized dreams, Luis is much like other boys his age in Malaga. From six years to ten, he went to a school taught by Catholic nuns, learned his catechism, to read and write a little, some arithmetic and some history. At ten, he was ready for work. (In Spain it is required by law that every child go to school until he is ten years old, but there are so many more children than schools that many boys and girls—no matter how eager—never get inside a schoolhouse).

If Luis had been a wealthy young Spaniard, or had an outstanding I. Q., he might have gone on to a private secondary school with his tuition paid for by his parents or a special scholarship fund provided by the state for very bright students. If he had been interested in crafts, mechanics or electronics, he might have applied (and then patiently waited his turn) to get into one of the good State-run trade schools in Malaga; or, he might have hired out immediately as an "apprentice" at about twenty cents a day, working and studying for from three to six years until he could qualify as an assistant or a "maestro" in such trades as carpentry, shoemaking, plumbing or metal working. (Luis' father is a *maestro mechanic,* earning twenty dollars a week, and his brother is an apprentice in the same factory, earning $4.50).

Many Spanish boys Luis' age without money, training or guidance "take to the streets" to make a living by shining shoes, running errands, selling gum and cigarettes or even peddling drinking water from a big earthenware jug for about one-quarter cent per long swallow. But Luis, in a poor, mountainous country where jobs are scarce and average wages lower than a dollar a day, is lucky enough to have a special talent. He can draw. "My big career started with Marilyn Monroe," Luis explains with a laugh. "But I could draw since I was four years old."

At four Luis was small for his age, always rather sickly,

LUIS HERNANDEZ, *Spain*

often underfed, but he could attract crowds on his little street by drawing pictures with chalk on the few smooth sections of cement in front of his house. He liked best to sketch the "Santa Semana" procession, the huge, four-day religious parade, held each Holy Week in Malaga and the other large cities in Spain. The procession, made up of heavy candle-lit, flower-decked floats carrying richly jeweled statues of the Blessed Virgin—one from each of the Catholic churches in town—winds through the streets from ten at night until two or three in the morning. Each float is preceded by a musical band and for four nights in a row, Holy Tuesday through Good Friday, the high, melancholy music, punctuated by drumbeats, reverberates and echoes through the whole city. The floats are carved, bejeweled and immensely heavy. Sometimes as many as 300 men sway under the weight of these thrones of the Virgin. Part of the procession consists of crowds of *penitentes,* members of parish marching clubs, dressed in flowing robes of black or white, tied at the waist with cord, and with high, pointed hoods that cover the whole face, except for slits at the eyes. Frequently along the route, which winds through both the business and residential sections of the city, a female *penitenta* will lean from a window, wailing out a traditional song of repentance for her sins, a melancholy, gypsylike song called a *sieta.*

Santa Semana is a dramatic religious spectacle, dating back to the Middle Ages, and it is also a social event in Malaga. Spanish ladies bring out their best black dresses, pearls, high combs and lace mantillas, to sit on folding chairs along the curbstones with their husbands, drinking lemonades and

[35]

watching the procession go past, dipping and swaying in its slow, fascinating rhythm.

Spain is a Catholic country, both traditional and superstitious in its many religious festivals and processions. Religious celebrations provide most of the entertainment and days-off for the working people. For instance, birthdays are rarely celebrated but the "name days," the feast day of the particular saint after whom one is named, is a time for parties and exchanging gifts. And the day of First Holy Communion is given both true pious observation and a full-dress treatment for every little boy and girl. For the occasion, girls wear the usual "miniature bride" costumes and little boys sport immaculate white outfits, ranging from long trouser and jacket ensembles with gold epaulets to a neat pair of white cotton pants and shirt, depending on the tastes and income of the family. After the solemn morning Mass, the children are allowed to parade through the streets for the day in full dress, visit friends and receive little gifts. On First Communion Day, these children are recognized and treated as celebrities by the whole town. And all through Spain, villages, schools, businesses celebrate *fiesta* periods by closing down every time a patron saint has a feast day.

The dramatic Santa Semana sketches are still favorites with Luis but he found, as he grew older, that he could draw almost anything with photographic accuracy. He only copied, though. At thirteen, he began studying art at night school but gave it up almost at once. "I don't like to be told what to do," he explains. "I didn't like all the talk about color and form so I just sat there copying pictures of Roman statues or drawing designs." One night a commercial photographer visited the school and hired Luis to work for him, tinting photo portraits at seventy-five cents a picture. Luis never went to school again. Instead, he worked two or three hours a day and earned enough "to fill my golden dream." At fourteen, he was earning enough money to go to the movies twice a day. The second-rate movie houses, hot and crowded, showed both Spanish and American movies —the latter with a censored, watered-down sound track in Spanish—and charged only eight cents admission. (In Spain, where both press and movies are heavily censored, 1955 was the first time in twenty-five years that uncut, undubbed foreign movies were shown in the country. Previously, when words and actions of the screen did not suit the censor's idea of morality, an actress' original speech, "Darling, I love you" might come out in dubbed-in Spanish as "Let us not be in haste, Señor!")

"The soft music in the movies is what I liked best," Luis explained. "I could think and feel away from everything. I didn't even tell my family where I went. One day after a movie, he bought a postcard of Marilyn Monroe advertising the movie *How to Marry a Millionaire*. Later, in his tiny bedroom, he copied the picture in black and white, enlarging it about ten times, but keeping it accurate in every detail. Next day, his sister, Maria, a part-time model in a dressmaking salon (very few clothes in Spain are bought in stores; most are made at home or custom-made by small dressmakers), had the picture framed and hung against the brown draperies of the dressmaker's workshop. A wealthy customer saw it and liked it. She asked Luis to draw her four children at the tremendous price of five dollars a picture. One customer brought another. Working only among wealthy families in Malaga and the tourists who crowd this picturesque

[37]

Mediterranean coastal section, Luis now sometimes does two black and white portraits a day and often earns as much as twenty-five dollars a week, more than his father, more than most teachers and policemen, in fact, more than most grown men in Spain, except for politicians, professional men and the very wealthy industrialists and landowners.

But though his family is proud of him, his brother and sisters are jealous, and his money has only made trouble at home for Luis. His brother says harshly, "You are only a good drawer, you will never be an artist."

Maria, fiercely hot-tempered yet possessive, said, "We do not even know where he keeps his money! I tell him to stay humble and to learn another trade but he has a big head. He won't even buy us a radio."

Luis, easily hurt and almost too shy to talk back, answered sullenly, "I pay five dollars a week for my board here. I am saving my money to go to art school in Madrid. And who wants a radio? It would cost sixty dollars and the house would be full of nothing but noise."

Maria answered sharply, "Work then, but don't think you are a genius. You can go to school if you get a scholarship —but I won't let you go anywhere before you are twenty. I am the mother here!"

"I'll run away," threatened Luis.

His sister became petulant and pleading. "You must support me. Who will take care of me in my old age?"

Luis shrugged and his handsome face was flushed and embarrassed. "You see why I go to the movies," he said abruptly.

Luis Hernandez is discontented, not only because he is a teen-ager growing up but also because he is a rarity in Spain:

in a poor country divided into the few "very rich" and the many "very poor," with a small proportion of the people between. He has *some* money and *some* talent—and doesn't know quite what to do with either. The 30,000,000 inhabitants of Spain are spread over a dry, rocky country, ribbed with mountains and shallow river beds empty six months of the year; fertile, irrigated and well-farmed areas are few. Several of the big cities are thriving and modern, Madrid, Seville, Barcelona and Valencia, for instance. But in these cities, while the center boulevards may hum with cars and buses and the bigger streets display public buildings graceful and elaborate and a few very modern, angular apartment buildings, the older parts of the town are little more than crooked, cobblestone lanes, with narrow, crowded houses, dimly lit and provided only with water carried in clay jugs from public water fountains scattered every few blocks throughout the city. Spain is primarily an agricultural country and, though there is some industry and manufacturing, especially in the north, most sophistication and modern living are focused in the cities only and these cities are compact, concentrated areas whose surroundings—and comforts—end abruptly.

In Madrid, for instance, the largest city in Spain and the center of the Spanish government, the big, elegant Palace Hotel stands as an efficient, luxurious, well-carpeted example of highest Spanish luxury. At seven-thirty in the morning, the giant lobbies hum with the sound of vacuum cleaners; neatly uniformed maids dust and clean; the switchboard is open for long-distance calls and the expensive luggage of international travelers is heaped near the revolving doors. In the breakfast room (a special room separate from the spacious dining room), a half-dozen waiters, immaculate even down to white cotton gloves, stand before the sideboard, ready to serve crisp rolls, still hot from the oven, iced orange juice and steaming coffee. The whole of the elegant breakfast scene is reflected in a full wall of mirrors. Outside, at this hour, the streets of Madrid are just coming to life—but it is the country life that is evident. They echo with the delicate *click-click* of the feet of tiny donkeys, heavily burdened or pulling the rickety farm wagons, loaded with produce from the nearby farms. Beside the carts walk the Spanish peasants, the men usually in shirt, tight black pants, straw-soled shoes and black beret, the women in faded, shapeless black, with a head-veil of black. Unlike those of the United States, Spanish cities have few prosperous suburbs and Madrid changes rapidly from crowded streets to flat, open country, dotted here and there with a low white farm house and a few small outbuildings and an occasional village.

Though Spain has several good seaports and is famous for its exports of sherry, olives, olive oil, oranges and cork, the farms of the country are mostly small, often just a few fields rented from a wealthy landowner who lives in a city most of the year. Every drop of water and inch of arable land is precious and orchards of fruit and olive trees are tended in carefully terraced slopes, sometimes curving up and down the mountainsides for miles. For the poor farmer, equipment may mean only a handplow, a cart and donkey—and a little white stone house with a cobblestone porch and an overhead arch of grape leaves. In many of the mountain villages there is no electricity at all and the clusters of houses, scrambled together up a slope, look as brown and dry as the clay from which they were made. Except in the northern part of Spain,

[40]

there is little good grazing land for beef cattle, but over the mountains feed 16,000,000 sheep, good for wool and mutton, and about a quarter as many goats, kept for milk and cheese. Frequently these flocks are watched over by an isolated teen-aged boy who spends hours a day alone on the mountainside, carrying a long carved staff and protected from wind, rain, sun and the chill weather of the winter months by a peak-hooded cape of coarse brown gunny sacking. And up and down the mountain slopes, in and out of the towns, over the brown Mediterranean sands go the million little brown donkeys, often jingling with bells and hung around the middle with red fringe, carrying the burdens of Spain.

The labor problem in Spain is not "unemployment" but "underemployment." Most people have something to do, but can't work hard enough to make an easy or even adequate living. In some of the fishing villages, families of eight must be fed on sixty cents a day and in the cities, construction workers rarely average more than eighty cents a day for a full nine or ten hours' labor. Bread is expensive, since Spain does not have much wheat-growing flatlands, and meat is not only expensive on the Spanish housewife's budget but in some areas very hard to buy at all. That leaves dairy products, fruits, vegetables and fish as main items of diet, and almost all food in the country is cooked in olive oil, thus giving a good diet substitute for meat, and leaving all over the land, between whiffs of orange blossoms or wet winter winds, the heavy, distinctive odor of hot, stale olive oil.

But in the Hernandez walk-up apartment, Luis is almost oblivious to what life is like in the rest of his country. Though he learned to read in school, he can't read well and never reads a book or even the daily paper. (Educated

[41]

Spaniards are often *very* well educated, familiar with the literature and history of their own country and the rest of the world, and often speaking two or three languages. Educated Spanish men love nothing more than a quiet hour in the afternoon, between six and seven, with a glass of white wine and a plate of cold shrimp and the local newspaper in some shady sidewalk cafe. On the other hand, about forty per cent of the people in Spain cannot read or write.)

"I just don't like to read," says Luis. "About twice a month or so, I walk over to the public library and spend a morning looking at magazines. I like the humor magazines and movie magazines best."

As a little boy, he read comic books about Tarzan and the Apes and "from Tarzan I got my first dreams of travel." But now Luis' dreams have turned from the land of Tarzan to Madrid, Paris and New York. The United States and Americans are currently very popular in Spain: Quantities of American magazines, weekly and monthly, are sold in Spain, the Spanish newspapers quote widely and warmly from the American press and many Spaniards feel a close kinship because of the great numbers of Spanish-Americans now American citizens. Others seem pleased that California and Florida are "just like Spain," with climate, architecture and life in the sun matching much of Spain. So great is American popularity right now that it is not infrequent, for instance, for a man on the street to say cordially to American tourists *"yo gusto mucho los Americanos"* ("I like Americans very much") or for a car with an American license plate to be greeted with a cheer as it passes through some remote Spanish village. (Also, work is currently in progress on four large bases for American jet-propelled fighters and bombers

[42]

near the town of Zaragozza, Madrid and at San Pablo and Moron de la Frontera, both near Seville, and also on a giant pipeline to carry jet fuel through the heart of Spain. While the U.S. Government has allotted $300,000,000 to be spent on these bases and has sent over thousands of advisers, technicians and workers, the major portion of the work is being done by Spaniards and the Spanish flag will fly over all bases. Some of the prosperity derived from the extra employment and the vast amount of money in use is already filtering down through Spanish economy.)

But again, Luis knows nothing of these airbases. His knowledge of Americans comes from the tourists he sees and the American movies which he now goes to at least five times a week. Though musicals and gangster movies are his favorites, he still firmly believes that he has a clear picture of American life. "I like the Americans for their freedom and independence. There is work and money for everyone. Every man is an individual. Everyone does what he likes." Luis even tries to dress like an American teen-ager. He dislikes fancy clothes (though he has a dark blue flannel suit for dances and fiestas) and usually wears moccasins, white T-shirts and well-pegged blue levis for which he pays three dollars a pair. Through the movies, too, he has some strong ideas about American juvenile delinquency and cannot understand it at all. "Why should anyone do such things—wrecking schools and stealing cars—in a country with so much work and money? Here a boy might steal if he was hungry or a gypsy might take a bicycle or something out of a garden. But no one from a good family would make trouble just for trouble." Even though he has never been in trouble of any kind, Luis is carefully watched at home: he never smokes,

[43]

sometimes drinks a bottle of beer on Sundays but never the local wine, both good and cheap. He has never driven a car and is usually in the apartment around midnight at the latest. Recently he stayed out with a group of boys till half-past twelve and his father told him that a second such mistake would mean no visits to the beach for a week.

But most often, during the day at least, Luis' life is independent and his plans are his own. Usually he lies in bed till ten, getting up only when the apartment is quiet and his aunt is out at the street market. For breakfast he has a piece of bread and marmalade and a glass of cold milk. The traditional Spanish breakfast is bread and marmalade and *"cafe con leche,"* a big cup of half coffee and half hot milk, heavily sugared. Since, except in the bigger cities, milk is rarely pasteurized, it is heated for breakfast coffee and made safe in the same process. In very poor homes, a family may start the day on bread dipped in olive oil.

In Spain, most stores—and schools—are closed from one o'clock until four, since the Spaniards who can afford it like both a long lunch and a chance for siesta. In the heat of the summer months, a nap behind cool, drawn shutters is imperative. The working day is then over at about eight o'clock in the evening, with the dinner hour—even for children— anywhere from ten to eleven and bedtime around midnight or later. Spaniards are night-lovers and families or men friends promenade or sit in cafes in the big cities till long after twelve o'clock.

To fill his days—when he is not doing portraits—Luis goes to the beach, wanders around the city streets with a boy friend and once in a while goes to the town museums or a local art exhibition. But Luis went to his first art show just three months ago. "To see good pictures depressed me," he said. "I guess I am not in love with painting. Somehow I think my vocation is not really painting. It is just something that comes out of my hands. Maybe I should be a wood carver. I don't think I understand really good art."

Two nights a week and most Saturday afternoons, Luis spends with his girl friend, a pretty, dark-haired sixteen-year-old named Maria Carmen. Luis blushes fiercely when he talks about her, partly because she is his first girl friend and partly because "love" is taken so seriously in Spain.

"She is not bold but very chaste," he began carefully. "I met her one night at a dance at a private club. Not really a club with a *clubhouse*—just a group of boys who put a little money together every once in a while to hire a little orchestra. Then we dance in the courtyard of someone's house. Maria Carmen came with her brother and he introduced us. I have known her now for about a year. Sometimes I go with her to an early movie. Or we just go for walks on Sunday—along the Avenida, to the docks or the lighthouse. Once in a while we go together to a relative's wedding or to a baptism. Sometimes we stop at a cafe for ice cream. But she is a *friend*," he insists, "not my *novia*."

The word *novia* (the male counterpart is *novio*) is an important word in Spain. It means "fiancée" and also "bride" and boys and girls, in all economic classes, are rarely allowed to spend time alone together until they are firmly—and with family approval—*novia* and *novio*. (Maria Carmen's family lets her spend time with Luis because he is a friend of her brother's but their type of dating is rare in this country.) Here there is almost no casual dating, driving around in cars together or staying out late, except with a chaperone, and even an unmarried girl in her twenties would not be seen alone with a man after ten o'clock at night.

A twenty-four-year-old girl living in Madrid, for instance, explained her social life this way: "On holidays or week-ends, groups of young men and women might get together to go to the beach, play tennis or go to the cinema. On Sunday afternoons, there might be tea dancing at a hotel. But I am usually home by eight o'clock, certainly not later than ten, and we go home in groups. At ten o'clock the front door to our apartment building is locked and I have to clap my hands for the *sereno* to come with his key. If I should go to the theater or a concert, I would go with my mother or an aunt. I am not engaged to be married, so I have never had a date alone. No man would expect it of me and I wouldn't want it. That is just our custom."

(A *sereno* or night watchman is, incidentally, a familiar sight in Spain after dark. This watchman is hired either by a large apartment building or by blocks of houses as a group, to watch over the street, guard doorways, etc., for about eighty cents a night. Occasionally, he is allowed to carry a revolver. He has a whistle to warn of thieves and a ring with keys to all apartments and houses and he also knows most of the tenants of his building by sight. In the old days, the *sereno* used to shout out the hours by calling, "Eleven o'clock and all's well," but now he makes his rounds in silence, waiting to be summoned by clapped hands to open doors.)

Among many wealthy families, a *senorita de compania*, a full-time chaperone, is hired, to watch over and escort society-aged daughters. A young Spanish man explained, "Love has great prestige here. In courtship, we usually have very pure, very idealistic relationships. In fact, with many Spanish girls, even a kiss is rare." (We went one evening to an elegant dinner dance in Valencia and most of the girls and boys were seated at tables with their families, as family groups rather than as dates, though a *novio* was sometimes seated at the table of his fiancée. The girls were all elaborately dressed in evening gowns, many with flowers pinned in their hair and the boys wore trim dark suits. The first course for dinner, a thick fish soup, was placed on the tables promptly at midnight and all through dinner and until four in the morning the couples chattered and danced to American dance tunes—but always under the watchful eyes of their parents and a tableful of relatives.)

Luis knows and sometimes visits with the parents of Maria Carmen, but he has never mentioned the girl to his own family. "My brother is moonsick about his own *novia* and my sister would be angry," he says. "What they don't know is fine with me."

In many parts of Spain, especially in the small villages, "courting habits" are so traditional that they form a definite pattern. For instance, a young man may see a girl on the street whom he admires. To attract her attention, he may walk up and down in front of her house for several evenings, carrying a note to her in his hand. If she sees him and wants to meet him, she first gets her parents' permission, then sends a message through a friend that she will accept the note. This note usually asks that the boy be allowed to speak with her through the grilled windows of the house. Such through-the-grill conversations may be carried on, evening after evening, for weeks or until the parents of the girl find out about the young man and are assured his intentions are honest. It is a marked step forward in the romantic relationship when the young man is asked into the house, to continue the visits under the watchful eyes of *madre y padre.* Only after a long friendship is the girl allowed to consider the young man her *novio.* All through Spain, on the warm, flower-scented evenings, it is possible to see boys and girls standing for hours, talking at a window, doorway or front gate. This courtship—called "plucking the turkey" because it takes so long—may go on for six or seven years or until the girl is in her early twenties and the boy twenty-five or older. Few have money to marry earlier.

No engagement rings are exchanged but traditionally the *novio's* mother gives the *novia* a bracelet and the boy himself may give her small presents from time to time, a necklace, a fan or some perfume. Traditionally also, the young man buys the wedding dress and provides the parlor furniture to begin housekeeping; the girl is expected to furnish the bedroom and kitchen and bring with her all the linens for the house, usually carefully embroidered and hand-sewn. In most families, relatives fill in with gifts for the house or small sums of money. Spain is still an acutely class-conscious country and, while most people are unusually courteous and respectful to everyone, there is little intermarriage "between classes." Class is decided both by money and by connections with "old families" but it is chiefly the barriers of education and the inability to earn money or make progress *without* an education that keep young people apart.

At sixteen, Luis Hernandez has no plans for marriage at all, but he enjoys his friendship with Maria Carmen and is as skilled at the art of the *piropo* as any sixteen-year-old in Malaga. The *piropo*—which means simply "compliment"— is an old, old Spanish custom, as much a part of the man-woman street flirtation as the American wolf whistle. But a *piropo* is always polite and respectful, and often poetic. It works this way: whenever a Spanish male passes a pretty girl walking alone on the street, he is free (in fact, bound by gallant tradition) to pay her a compliment, whatever comes to his mind as best suiting the girl and her attractions. The girl does not acknowledge the compliment in any way, not even by a smile, but she would be disappointed if every walk didn't earn a *piropo* or two. Some of the most average flatteries are simply *"Que guapa!"* meaning "What a beauty!" or *"Madre mia, no puedo a creer!"* —"Mother mine, I can't believe it." A young Spaniard told me seriously that the most perfect, spontaneous *piropo* he ever heard was given by a friend of his who spotted a pretty girl coming down the street. "What beauty!" he sighed to her. "You are more graceful than Manolete on his greatest day in the bullring!" (Manolete is the great modern bullfight hero, famous for his skill and style.) Such exaggerated compliments are not only enjoyed, but expected. The Spaniards are dramatic, self-aware people with great humor but highly excited by life. Each Spaniard, no matter how poor, is able to see himself as a hero—and to treat the girl of his choice as a heroine. Therefore, love and the affairs of love are always important. On warm summer nights, and even in the bright sun of high noon, the streets of Malaga are a-hum with *piropos*. When the exaggerated compliments do *not* come, the girls are disappointed.

Not many blocks from Luis' apartment stands the giant bullring of Malaga, a circular three-story arena of red brick and rough stone, as familiar a piece of architecture as the steepled Catholic churches or majestic cathedrals that dominate every town in Spain. For centuries, the bullfight has been as popular in Spain as baseball is in the United States; it draws huge crowds, makes national heroes of the top bullfighters and frequently pays them more than even such major league players as Mickey Mantle. A good, popular bullfighter, or matador, can earn 150,000 pesetas ($3,750) in one afternoon and may fight as often as fifty times a season. The great Manolete, gored to death in 1947, was paid as high as $30,000 for one afternoon's work with the bulls and had earned $4,000,000 before he died in the little white bullring in the town of Linares, just a few hours after he had been mortally wounded by the horn of a dying bull. It is little wonder that most of the boys in Spain dream at some time in their lives of becoming matadors. But it takes great courage and skill to face the sharp horns of the bull, alone before crowds of thousands, and there are usually no more than three or four top matadors in Spain at one time.

Each year, the bullfight season begins in March or April, right after Easter, and ends in October. And each year the bigger cities of Spain hold "fiesta weeks," marked by parades, huge carnivals and a full week of *corridas* or bullfights, starting promptly at five or six each afternoon, depending on the heat of the day. This year, as always, the fiesta opened in Malaga, with the bullring jammed; three dollars for seats in the sun *(sol)* and as much as twenty-five dollars for seats in the shade *(sombra)*. The judge's box, in the top tier of seats above the ring, was crowded with a selection of especially pretty Malaguenians—mostly the daughters and relatives of city officials—dressed in pastel summer dresses, but heavy with make-up and wearing the traditional high comb, lace mantilla and flower behind the ear. The air glistened with

[50]

noise, color and excitement and the town was as tense as any baseball town the day the World Series opens. For a week, Malaga thought and talked nothing but "bullfight." Even though soccer (called *futbol* by the Spaniards) has become increasingly popular, crowding as many as 100,000 shouting, handkerchief waving spectators into the Royal Madrid Stadium, bullfighting is still the most popular sport in Spain.

But not with Luis Hernandez. "I don't like the crowds," he explains. "I don't like the noise and the push. And I don't like to see animals killed. I used to go when I was younger but I have other interests now."

Against another of Spain's great traditions, Luis is also a rebel. In a Catholic country where religious festivals mark every month of the year and Sunday morning finds the streets crowded with black-veiled women devoutly on their way to Mass, Luis has decided he no longer wants to go to church. His old aunt, who is an ardent churchgoer herself, simply shrugs. "Young people get such ideas but they come around," she says.

"I can explain myself," Luis began (with religion, as with so many things, he is almost too shy to express himself.) "I am a Catholic and I believe in God, but I don't go to church and I don't believe in priests. All my friends are indifferent, too. When we were little, everyone made such a fuss about it. The day I made my First Communion I wore a white suit and was paraded through the streets and everyone acted like I was a saint. Now I am awfully skeptical." (Luis was, of course, speaking only for the limited number of boys and girls with whom he was associated. The majority of the young people of Spain adhere closely to their belief in the Catholic Faith.)

[51]

But at all the colorful religious festivals, Luis is always on hand, both for the spectacle and to be with his friends. (For instance, he went to watch the annual "blessing of the sea" ceremony in the fishing village of Torremolinos. Late at night, carrying lighted candles and chanting hymns, the entire village followed behind a raised statue of the Blessed Virgin decked with flowers. At the edge of the Mediterranean, while the waves splashed around the feet of the statue, the parish priest blessed the waters and asked the Virgin for safety and prosperity for the fishermen for the coming year.) "That is religion, of course," said Luis. "But I like the ceremony for the beauty and the color, not for what I believe."

And what is it like for a teen-ager to live in a country governed by a dictator? About this, Luis has little to say. The bitter Spanish Civil War, in which 2,000,000 Spaniards were killed, was over in 1939, before Luis was born. Since the war, and all of Luis' lifetime, just one man has been in power in Spain. Now the picture of Generalissimo Francisco Franco, elaborately uniformed and neatly mustached, appears in most of the bars, restaurants and shops in Spain and occasionally one sees the legend, *"Viva Franco! Viva España!"* scrawled in a city square or painted along a country wall. But on the whole, life seems free and easy politically for most Spaniards. Both press and radio are controlled, with insistence on a minimum of criticism and a maximum of praise for the present government. Franco is undisputed head of that government and, though Spain has a lawmaking body somewhat equvalent to our Congress, most of the politically powerful men hold office by appointment. But the country is free of the heavy propaganda, patriotic posters, parades and rallies and the emphasis on "the state" that so clearly marks other such governments as Jugoslavia and East Germany. Right after the Civil War, a youth group called the *"Frente de Juventudes"* ("Youth Front") was organized, complete with uniforms, regular meetings and clubhouses and obligatory membership for both boys and girls. "But," explained an older Spaniard who had fought through the Civil War with Franco's forces, "Hitler and Mussolini, with their Nazi and Fascist youth groups, made this kind of thing very unpopular in Spain. Spaniards refused to send their children to the youth meetings. No one did anything about it and the groups have almost died out. In a few places, the groups still exist, mostly as social groups. Nothing more." Luis insists he has never even heard of the *Frente de Juventudes*.

Generalissimo Franco is generally popular in Spain (though in such a regime, opposition is usually silenced harshly and early) and many people believe that, when the time is right, Franco will bring about the re-instatement of a royal family in Spain, with Prince Juan Carlos of Bourbon as the First King of Spain. Prince Juan Carlos, a handsome, curly-headed teen-ager, now studying in Madrid, will reach the age of twenty-one in 1959. It is almost certain that *"El Caudillo"* ("The Leader") Franco will keep his position as Spanish dictator until that time. However, in recent months, general transportation strikes in Barcelona, as a protest against a rise in fares on street cars and buses, and demonstrations by University students in Madrid show that some dissatisfaction with the government definitely exists.

We saw Generalissimo Franco at a bullfight in Malaga, sitting in the president's box and surrounded by male dignitaries. The streets of the town had been hung with red and yellow Spanish flags for his visit and a giant triumphal arch of flowers was erected over the main street for his autocade. However, at the bullfight, Franco appeared in a simple gray business suit, without a uniformed guard in sight. He looked brisk, suntanned and benign, accepted only a small ovation from the crowd and then waved good-naturedly to "get on with the *corrida*." In fact, the appearance of Ava Gardner at a previous fight seemed to cause more fevered excitement.

A newspaperman from Malaga tried to explain Franco's appeal for Spaniards in this way: "He has been good for Spain in this time in our history," he said. "After the Civil War here, we were a broken and dangerous country. Without him, there would have been more chaos and more bloodshed. Franco's regime has been like a cast on a broken leg. As a country, we are almost well, and we believe that when we are strong enough, Franco will take off the cast."

When he is twenty, Luis Hernandez, like all young Spanish men, will have to serve in the army for two years. "I'll be glad to go," he says with conviction. "The army tries to send boys as far away from their home towns as they can. Maybe it will give me a chance to see something besides these same streets. I would like to see and do new things. I just don't *want* old things anymore. I don't like *old* streets, *old* churches, the *old* ways of living. I think I even hate the old Roman ruins around Malaga because people make so much of them. I like my country but I want a new kind of life, I want to be *myself*."

Though he is so quick to criticize his present life, Luis— like many young Spaniards—does not want the responsibility of figuring out how to change it. Perhaps to earn a living

[54]

or get an education in a poor country is problem enough; perhaps the young Spaniards do not want added responsibilities.

Luis smiled and seemed almost relieved that this "thinking" about himself and his life was over. "I have no real dream," he said. "I will work, learn to speak English—and then what? Time will tell me what to do."

3

FELICITY CONNOLLY

Ireland

"I THINK," said Felicity Connolly, "that students of my age in Ireland are for the most part intelligent but not very well-informed. We are amusing and generous but very off-hand about money. Most of us study hard—but we don't know yet what to be. Maybe we are like young people everywhere, but somehow I think we are less sure of ourselves."

We were sitting that day in the waiting room of Sion Hill Academy, a private school for girls, set in a sprawling, bright green garden in a Dublin suburb. The room was crowded with big plush chairs and sofas, every hand-crocheted anti-macassar neatly in place. Late afternoon sun glinted off rows of gilt-framed holy pictures and in one corner of the room, a jar of spring daffodils and a flickering candle stood before a small statue of the Blessed Virgin. Teachers, nuns of the Dominican Order, hurried in and out, their black and white robes fluttering. It was four o'clock in the afternoon and school was over for the day. A few students, ranging from five years to eighteen, still chattered and giggled in the hallways and from somewhere far down the scrubbed, chilly corridors came the smell of fresh coffee.

Felicity sat straight and tall on a plush sofa, feet together, neat, chapped hands folded in her lap. She looked slim and pretty in the school uniform, a jumper of light blue wool, white blouse and black blazer with the school crest. "No make-up" is the rule of the school but Felicity's elfin face is naturally pink-cheeked and her eyes bright. She was eager to talk but shy. "We are all convent girls here," she explained. "I hope what I can tell you is interesting enough."

Felicity has lived in Dublin for half her life and started school at Sion Hill when she was just a little girl. She is sixteen now and moved from County Cork with her family when she was just eight. Now the Connollys—Felicity, three sisters and a young brother of ten—live in a rambling, nine-room brick house on a shaded lane in the Dublin suburb of Blackrock. In Ireland, almost every suburban or country house is given a name with a nameplate on the gate. "Rose Cottage," "Tudor House" or "St. Anne's," for example. The

Connolly house is dubbed with the name "Clohanes"—"but we all think it is such a plain name that we just call our house 'Number 12,' " explained Felicity.

And Number 12 is a busy place. All five children are still in school and Mr. Connolly leaves early each morning for downtown Dublin, where he is a bank manager. Felicity, the oldest in the family, gets about eighty-five cents a week allowance but likes to save those six shillings "for sweets and personal things," so she starts early and walks the long, tree-lined block to her first nine-thirty class. In Ireland, education is compulsory till the age of fourteen (though in some poor, over-crowded city areas, children do not have the shoes or warm clothing to get to school) but Sion Hill is a tuition school, as are many of the better schools in Ireland, and Felicity works and studies as if she means to make every shilling of her tuition count.

"I study so hard you might thing I *knew* what I wanted to be after I graduate," said Felicity with a laugh. "But I am not at all sure. So far, I have had four years of cookery and domestic studies here. I might go on to a special school to study hotel management. I think I would like that. And I think I could find a job in Ireland." (About one-third of this little green island's "foreign income" comes from the thousands of tourists who flock here each year, mostly emigrated Irishmen returned home for a visit, or people whose parents and grandparents were born here and who want to see "the old country.")

To be certain that she "finds a job" some day, Felicity is in school six hours a day and studies at least two hours every night. Besides history, geography, Math, English, French, Christian Doctrine and domestic science, she is now in her tenth year of studying the Irish language. In Ireland, every street sign and country road marker is printed in two languages: English and Gaelic (Irish). Students must be taught Gaelic in school, parts of most newspapers are printed in Irish, while radio programs and local theaters present plays completely in Irish several times a year. To hold a job in the Irish government or civil service, one must be able to speak and write both English and Gaelic.

This determined drive to bring back Gaelic as part of the island's speech is symbolic of the little island's struggle to "stay Irish." At one time, centuries ago, Gaelic was the only language spoken in the land. Then, when England took over the island as one of its colonies, demanding high taxes and loyalty to the crown as its price for this privilege, one of the many unjust laws levied on the Irish was the decree that made the speaking of Gaelic illegal. (At one time, too, it was considered "treason" for the Irish to use the name "Ireland" in speech or song. Hence they nicknamed their beloved little country such things as "The Wise Old Woman," "My Dark Rosaleen" and "Cathleen ni Houlihan," and spoke and sang of it as they wished). Thus, English became the official language. Over the years, English also became the most commonly used language and most children growing up never heard—and never learned—their native tongue. The Gaelic language almost died out.

But from 1916 to 1921, Ireland fought a bitter, bloody war for independence from England and as soon as this freedom was won, determined to re-educate the Irish people in Gaelic. In some tiny farm communities or in remote fishing villages on the rocky coast, there are still Irishmen who speak Gaelic naturally. But most young Irish people, like Felicity, study ten hard years or more to master the difficult alphabet, pronunciation and vocabulary, completely unlike everyday English.

This "need to be Irish" seems to affect everyone living on the little island today. It is fewer than forty years since the Irish rebellion against England was won. Naturally, many of the people who fought and suffered are still alive. Scenes of savage fighting—the famous Post Office on O'Connell Street and the bridge on Lower Mount Street—where dozens of Irish patriots died are still part of everyday Dublin city life. These landmarks of heroes are in evidence throughout Ireland. Everyone knows, as if it were a short yesterday, where the battles were fought.

And to keep these war memories very much alive, part of the island of Ireland is still not Irish: the *south* of Ireland, made up of twenty-six counties, is ruled by Irishmen alone, but the *north* of Ireland, a small area of six counties, is still part of the British Isles and flies the British flag! Thus, in this tiny island, people of the same blood and heritage are not truly united. In fact, a boundary line or frontier, manned by British and Irish custom officials, physically separates the land and it is impossible to drive from the north to the south without a passport or identity papers to cross the border. In the south, the tri-color flag of yellow, white and green flies proudly; in the north, pictures of Queen Elizabeth grace the taverns and hotel lobbies and before soccer matches in the big northern city of Belfast, it is not the Irish National Anthem that is played but England's *God Save the King*. It is because of this fierce love of country that southern Irish students, such as Felicity, do not mind

[60]

years of studying a language which could never be understood outside their own tiny island.

When there is work to be had, the Irish are hard working people, beginning the day early. Felicity is up at seven-thirty, for a breakfast sturdy enough to start a farmhand off for a day in the fields. If the family budget permits, Irishmen usually choose a hot breakfast—perhaps rashers (a special Irish bacon like our ham), eggs with grilled tomatoes, bread and butter, marmalade and a pot of tea with milk. This wind-swept island is truly an "emerald isle," with the grass and shrubs kept green from frequent rains and sea mists, but the climate ranges from bitter in the winter to chilly other months of the year, except for the three months of summer. Hence, though Spaniards and Italians and others from southern countries with more gentle climates can start the day on bread and coffee, the Irish need more nourishment. And the big meal of the day, the "meat and potatoes meal," falls at noontime, with school children and most businessmen rushing home for dinner and a two-hour break. There is one bicycle for overy three persons in Dublin—a high population in wheels—and at noontime and after work, the streets are crowded with bicycles, whizzing and zipping through motor traffic. I have even seen teen-agers guiding a bike with one hand and holding a book in the other, in the rush of traffic on Dublin's downtown O'Connell Street!

"I always hurry home at noontime and sometimes I help make the dinner," Felicity explained. "Until February last, we had a full-time maid but now we just get along with morning help to clean up things. I'm not a good cook yet and just try simple things—pork steak, potatoes and some kinds of tarts. But most Irish girls learn how to cook at least a little."

Irish tea time—from about five to seven in the evening—is one of the most pleasant times of the day. Then the whole family sits down to a heavy tea, usually the final meal, of such things as scrambled eggs, cold meat, fruit, bread and jam or cake—and a big pot of tea with milk and sugar. Many countries have distinctive food customs: the Frenchman likes a cognac or glass of wine at a sidewalk cafe; a German may prefer a big cup of coffee with pastry at four o'clock; an Italian will choose a tiny, bitter cup of *cafe espresso* at an outdoor coffee bar; and an American might look for a refresher in an iced soft drink. But the daytime break for an Irishman is a cup of tea, preferably at home, by his own fireside, with a heavily lined, embroidered "tea cosy" covering the pot while the tea steeps. Very few Irish homes have central heating, so the evening fire in the hearth (coal and wood are expensive, so a lit fire is a treat) and the pot of tea are truly the center of the family.

So important is a good cup of tea to the average Irishman that I saved an interesting letter from a Dublin evening newspaper on the proper methods of making tea. The letter was written in answer to several others to the newspaper on the same subject:

> From 2,000 years of experimenting there have evolved various methods of making tea; obviously no one is under any obligation to follow one particular method . . . but I wish to answer a question frequently asked—what is recognized by expert tea tasters as the best way of making tea.
>
> I am aware that certain people of the world add lemon

to the tea liquor. We in this country add sugar and milk. The Estonians flavor their tea with jam. The Tibetans, the greatest tea drinkers in the world, mix together butter, salt and soda and add this to the tea liquor for flavor. But in no country does anyone tamper with the dry leaf.

And now this question of the dry pot. The full flavor and aroma of tea is only released by boiling water. Tea is a plant and very quickly absorbs moisture. If the tea leaves are put in a wet pot, a certain quantity immediately becomes soggy and moisture laden, thus losing the effect of boiling water on them; these leaves do not infuse, resulting in much good tea being wasted."

"I'll admit that right now I *think* more about cooking than I actually cook," said Felicity. "But like everyone, I do like a good cup of tea." In Ireland, a damp country where both hearthfires and incomes are sometimes low, this "bit of fire and a cup of tea" comfort is often the high spot of the whole day. Most Irishwomen, from teen-agers up to grannies, go through the winter months with the backs of their legs rough and chapped from the combination of wet weather outside and toasting at the hearthside inside.

Unemployment is always a problem in Ireland. In a few suburbs and in the country, there are large, comfortable homes and some people (chiefly professional people or land-owners in this agricultural country) manage to live well and with security. In fact, there are still some castlelike homes set in acres of estate, complete with outbuildings, stables and staffs of servants. But too many Irishmen pinch along without work or skimp on a laboring man's salary of about fifteen to twenty dollars a week.

After fourteen years of age, it is permissible for young people to take jobs in industry or business, either as apprentices or on full time. Newspapers run frequent ads such as this: "Wanted—competent girl to help in bakery shop. No one over 17 need apply." In many cases, big families and low wages make it necessary for young people to take jobs whenever and wherever they can, to help out at home. Just outside the big city of Belfast, in a small country village, I met a typically good-natured but hard-pressed boy of fifteen who was smiling over his new good luck: he was the oldest of seven children and as a farmhand, his father earned seventeen dollars a week. The boy had just found a job tending chickens at a large, English-owned farm, working six days a week, from eight in the morning till five at night, for eighty cents a day. And he was proud of this chance to quit school and begin to help his family.

Many young Irishmen, industrious and eager for employment, find jobs so hard to get that nearly half a million, out of the total population of less than 3,000,000 in the south, have drifted across the Channel to find work in English factories or doing lesser laboring jobs.

"In this school, we are students who spend most of our time studying," explained Felicity earnestly, "but even if we wanted to, most of us couldn't find work. The shops have too many grown-up people looking for jobs to bother with teen-agers. I did have a job once—last Christmas. I took phone calls at a chiropodist's office in our suburb because he happened to be especially busy. I worked for sixteen hours in all and earned about six dollars—or about thirty-five cents an hour, which wasn't bad. I used the money to buy Christmas presents and one or two gramaphone records."

Of course, for young people all over this island—and especially in a big capital city such as Dublin—life is not all study or hard work. Riding and fox hunting are major sports in Ireland but both, unfortunately, are chiefly "sports for the gentry," and it is usually only the wealthy and titled Irishman who can afford or is allowed to ride with the hunt. For the average Irish teen-ager, the most popular amusements are field sports, movies and dancing.

"We have many good sports here at school, and I play them all," said Felicity. "Tennis, field hockey and net ball. And I belong to the Girl Guides, rather like your Girl Scouts. We meet every Thursday during the winter and in good weather we hike. Once a year we go to camp somewhere out in the country." Next to soccer, hurling is the nation's favorite sport—a game much like ice hockey but played on a grass field—and a big hurling match can draw as many as 80,000 people to Croke Park in Dublin. Soccer and hurling players are the celebrities of the sports page, as admired and well followed as top baseball players and prize fighters in the United States.

"I love the theater, too," Felicity explained, "but can't afford to go too often." (Dublin is the home of the famous Abbey Theatre and Abbey Players but the six shillings admission would use up her entire allowance for a week). "And I go to the movies only when a good one comes along, even though everyone here is movie-mad."

Movie theaters in Ireland are different from ours in two ways: first, they are theaters plus restaurants, tea rooms, bars and waiting rooms, all in one building. It is possible to have a full dinner—or just a soft drink downstairs—at any time during the show. Secondly, theaters are so popular and so few that it is often impossible to get in at all. On Sundays, all seats are sold in advance and reserved, and wealthy

[65]

families sometimes book the same seats a year ahead. On most week nights, the line outside the box-office usually means a twenty-minute or half-hour wait for seats; on Friday and Saturday night, a boy and girl on a date may wait out on the sidewalk, chatting and shuffling to keep warm, for as long as two hours. But the theaters are never empty.

"There just aren't enough 'dreams' to go round," a newspaperman commented. "Life is too strict in this country for young people and there just isn't enough to do—so they live from one change of movie program to the next."

And life in Ireland *is* strict for young people. Partly, a lack of money keeps life simple and hard working. And partly, this is due to the influence of the Catholic Church. For centuries, while Ireland was dominated by England, it fought for religious freedom and now—as a free country—it has impressed some hard rules upon itself. There is, for instance, strict censorship on movies, books and magazines. Every movie must pass a board of censors and "objectionable" parts are cut from the film. Sometimes such cuts are made skilfully but occasionally a whole scene is simply left unfinished or a chapter may drop out of a movie without explanation, never to be seen again. In the same way, a book may be censored right out of the bookshops. (One day I saw a copy of Graham Greene's *The Quiet American* in a bookshop window. When I went in to buy it the next day, it had been "censored" from the shelves.) Since Ireland is a small country, many of its printed things, except for daily papers, come from outside the country and most of its magazines come from England. Irishmen are no longer surprised when a favorite magazine does not show up for a week—the issue may have been rejected by the censorship board for a number of reasons. Perhaps a layout of a movie star showed too much bare leg; perhaps there was an article too critical of the Catholic Church, or too much in favor of certain international personalities. Many Irish people are ashamed of this censorship—but no one seems to know what to do about it.

Great emphasis is put on "proper behavior" in this country, especially among young people, and very few teenagers begin to date at all until they are eighteen or nineteen. "This is because we are convent educated," Felicity explained, feeling that statement covered the matter.

"I wouldn't go out alone with boys," she went on, "but I am allowed to go out with a group of young people. I can stay out until ten o'clock, if my parents know where I am: later, of course, for special occasions. I have danced only a little, in private homes—and, of course, we have dances here at school." (At school dances, mostly late afternoon get-togethers in the school gym, no boys are allowed. Music comes from a victrola and the girls dance with each other, waltzing or jitterbugging around in school uniforms and seeming to have a good, relaxing time.)

Public dance halls are very popular, but mostly with the older, young-twenties crowd and many young people go in groups, boys and girls separately. In-town dance halls charge about ninety cents per person, while in the suburbs, where the decoration and atmosphere is like that of a small-town country club, admission may be as high as $1.25 apiece, with music by a full orchestra and little tables for soft drinks or ices.

"Teddy boys," a type of juvenile delinquent peculiar to England and some of the bigger cities of Ireland, are often the terror of Dublin dance halls. Many public places have

[67]

signs over the ticket booths reading: "Gentlemen in teddy boy costume not admitted." "Teddy boys" are a type of young hoodlum who likes to travel in gangs, specialize in minor rioting and thievery, roughing up other teen-agers and generally causing trouble. All this roughhouse conduct seems even more peculiar because the boys invariably wear "teddy boy" clothing, patterned after elegant gentlemen in the time of Edward VII: long-tailed coats with velvet collars, pleated or ruffled white shirts, narrow, rain-pipe trousers and hair worn rather long and waved in Lord Byron fashion. These teen-agers may be delivery boys, factory workers, shop clerks, etc., by day, but at night, elegant and dangerous, they prefer to prowl the town in gangs. In Dublin, for instance, they once stopped all traffic on busy O'Connell Street by forming a human chain across the roadway; in dimly-lit side streets, they liked to wait for anyone coming to pick up his parked car—then offer an ultimatum: five-dollar payment for "parking charges" or a beating on the spot.

In all the weeks I spent in Dublin, I saw only one teddy boy myself. And he was alone, meekly waiting in line to get a ticket to a cowboy movie. But his clothes (all obviously very expensive) would have suited the most elegant blood of several decades ago. His ruffled shirt was white and starched, his hair carefully waved and curled. Alone, he didn't look dangerous, only self-conscious and a little scared. Teddy boy gangs have never become the menace in Dublin that they are in more crowded, cosmopolitan London. The tough, hot-tempered Irish have a way of their own of handling such delinquency and often a potential teddy boy terror has gotten a worse beating than he intended to give. One teen-aged boy told me his older brother had joined a teddy boy gang "but my mother took the stick to him and he gave it up."

In explaining her own social life, Felicity said a little defensively. "We like to have a good time here, too, but we would just never go in for steady dating as apparently you do in the United States." Whether because of the "tight" social life, or because it is just too expensive for most young people to dream of starting a home, Ireland has the lowest marriage rate in the world, with many people never able to start an independent home. Naturally, with a low marriage rate, the birth rate is also low and the little island is one of the few places in the world where people are getting fewer and fewer! About a hundred years ago, the population was about two and a half times as high as it is now.

"I haven't traveled much, except through Ireland, but I've heard a lot about other countries from my parents," said Felicity. "When my mother was a young girl, she worked as a nursemaid for a wealthy family, who took her to Portugal. Later, when she got married, she and my father went back to Portugal for a honeymoon. I'd like to see those "sun countries" and, above all, I think I'd pick Spain. I have read a lot about it."

Reading is a major hobby with Felicity—mostly historical books and war novels—and her second hobby is collecting the autographs of well-known authors. When she was fifteen, she wrote to Somerset Maugham, telling him how much she liked his books, and the gracious old author sent back a warm thank-you note and his autographed picture.

Dublin, though the capital of southern Ireland, is different from the rest of the country. It is the graceful, sophisticated city, built outwards from the banks of that low, gray river, the Liffey. Some midcity sections are crowded with moldering, ancient slum buildings where families may be living six to a room. But its main street, O'Connell Street, is jammed with double-decker buses, department stores, four-story movie theaters and little snack restaurants with juke boxes, neon lights and names such as The Santa Fe and The Broadway. Around some of the small in-town parks, well-cared for and green the year round, stand graceful Georgian houses, old but well-preserved, with the calm, last-century architecture still seen in Philadelphia and Baltimore. The suburbs start with big old houses, hedged into sprawling gardens, and merge into raw new buildings—square, overly-trim houses, mostly in pebbledash or painted stucco, each fronted by a bit of green lawn and a gate. But outside of Dublin, the queen city, most of southern Ireland is made up of small towns, villages or open countryside.

In most country towns, the main street is built extra wide' to accommodate the cattle on market day. On that day, the center of town is crowded with the healthy, shaggy brown and white cows (much of Ireland's income is derived from the export of beef and dairy products to England), tethered along the sidewalk, and the farmers come to town with low cartloads of pigs for sale, each scrubbed till it looks like a pink, glistening toy. From little pubs, on market day, come the sounds of singing, often to the accompaniment of a thin, high violin. Ireland is not a country of outdoor food markets or outdoor cafes but the street scene of market day is as gay as a carnival and the country lanes for miles around are crowded with farmers, walking their cattle to and from town.

Though much of the countryside is simply bright green, lightly wooded and softly hilly, Ireland also has some areas of barren wastes and stark mountain peaks. We drove late one winter afternoon to the west coast town of Donegal, through miles and miles of lonely valley between bare mountains, on toward a low light that was both the setting sun and the open sea. Along the rocky seacoasts, the fishing villages are few and small. One Sunday night in December, we followed a roadsign to a town with a wonderful name: Killybegs. At seven-thirty, the town was shut tight, with a wind whipping off the sea and not a person in sight except the occasional head that appeared at a lighted window, curious at the sound of a car in the night. In these villages, women often spend time at the hearthside, knitting and weaving, and some of the fine "cottage industries" products find their way into the smartest shops as far away as Paris and New York.

Throughout the countryside, most of the older cottages are long, one-story buildings, climbing with vines around the gateways and thatched low, with heavy roofs of thick, tight straw. "Peat"—thick squares of turf soil cut from the earth and dried—is still the chief fuel in the country and near every farm cottage is a pile of hay for the cattle and a pile of turf bricks for the fireplace inside. Turf bogs spot the country side, great emptied areas filling with water, the sides of the pond showing clearly the squared mark of the turf cutter's blade. In most of Ireland, the people dress exactly as most farm-town Americans do, except perhaps with more rain-coats, umbrellas and headkerchiefs for the wet weather. But in remote areas, especially along the west sea coast, older women still do wear—over the head, round the shoulders and down to the ankles—the "old plaid shawl" in red and green, made so famous in Irish folk music. The more popular costume, however, is a blouse with a full ankle-length skirt in black and huge, wrap-around shawls in brown and beige.

The coastal landscape is rough and wildly beautiful, strewn with rocks and lashed by winds from the sea (no part of this little island is more than sixty miles from the sea coast.) Incongruously, a few tall palm trees tower over the rough fields, fronds tossing in the wind.

In the very heart of the island, in the farm country in the north, we visited an old farmhouse, a low, stone whitewashed building over two hundred years old. Here, remote from the main roads, the work of the whole farm was done by men and horses, without electricity or motors. The kitchen, high-ceilinged and smoke-stained, was the main room of the house, with a sink and pump in one corner, a huge table and cracked leather chairs before the fire. Two giant shepherd dogs roamed in and out of the house at will, sometimes leaving to herd cattle in the nearby meadows, sometimes settling before the fire, to rest and dry their long coats. The hearth-fire, a heap of turf smoldering on the floor without andirons, smoked and cracked and filled the air with a blue pungence. A giant black pot which could be elevated high or low over the fire by hooks was swung to one side and a kettle of tea water bubbled close to the fire. The scene was as majestic and simple as something from the Middle Ages.

In the deep countryside, many Irishmen are still charmingly affected by their belief in fairies or "wee folk" and certain shadowed hollows along every country road are rumored to be haunted, bewitched or just plain unlucky. Our host at the farmhouse was a firm believer in magic, though, as he explained, "the priest in the village won't have me saying it." But as a younger man (he was then in his late eighties) he had made his living going from farm to farm and around the village fairs, curing ringworm in cattle with his "gift." He simply spat on his finger, touched the ailing animal and in a few weeks, he insisted, it was cured. "I have the magic in me," he said, "as does every other man whose name begins with Mc. Everybody knows it."

Felicity Connelly, at sixteen, educated and living in Dublin, is—of course—a product of modern Ireland. But this little island is never far from its troubled past. And to understand the people, it is necessary to understand something of what happened in Ireland in the past centuries—or even the last decades. Why are jobs so hard to find? Why is it not a country as prosperous as England or America? The answers are harsh but simple. For years the island was ruled by invaders. First the Danes, then the Anglo-French, then—until 1921—the English. In 1840, a great potato famine swept the country; thousands of Irishmen emigrated to the United States and Canada. Less lucky thousands stayed home to die. Later, English laws kept Irishmen from owning land and making just profits on their farms or in business. Then came the Irish war of rebellion against England, followed by a devastating civil war. Economically, Ireland fell farther and farther behind the rest of the English-speaking world. One melancholy poet described it as "a sleepwalker falling off the face of Europe."

In time, investment of foreign money and the development of industry may change all this but right now, as a farm country, with few natural resources and little to sell the outside world, the island has become less and less important, except in the hearts of the thousands of people who left to earn a living somewhere else. (There are more people of

Irish derivation in New York City, for instance, than in the whole of southern Ireland.) Yet the Irish still on their own soil are fiercely proud of the Irish who have left home to "make good." Comedian Jackie Gleason, song writer George M. Cohan, actress Grace Kelly and many others are all mentioned, almost defiantly, as "Irish."

"Our young people," the Irish often point out sadly, "are Ireland's most valuable export." But hard-working, bright-eyed Felicity Connolly is a good example of the sturdy little country still left behind.

4

KRISHNA DASWANI KHUBCHAND

Gibraltar

Round the world, Gibraltar is known simply as "The Rock." It rises almost 1400 feet above the water, to stand guard over the narrow stretch of sea where the Atlantic Ocean joins the Mediterranean. It is geographically a part of Spain, joined to the mainland by a rocky strip. It flies a British flag and looks out over a few miles of water to the close shores of North Africa.

[75]

In the rough waters of the port, British Navy ships lie at anchor but the freight and passenger boats hoist the flags of every nation. High up on the great rock, camouflaged in the barren stretches covered with scrub bushes and tiny yellow flowers, are hidden the powerful gun batteries that make Gibraltar one of the strongest and most famous defense positions on earth.

In the town of Gibraltar, old and overcrowded, the narrow streets climb crookedly up the rock, with shops and houses jammed together. Crowds push and jostle each other on the one-lane sidewalks and out onto the streets. A constant breeze whips in from the sea and brilliant yellow and blue Chinese pajamas, heavy damask bedspreads and colored satin kimonos twist and turn on their hangings outside the shops. Cuckoo clocks, walking dolls, lace fans and embroidered slippers are set outside the doorways to attract buyers and, like an eternal carnival, tourists and sailors from all over the world swarm through the town, fill the bars and bargain for souvenirs, in the few hours they have to spend on shore.

From nine each morning until nine-thirty each night, Krishna Khubchand works in his shop, often standing in the doorway to stare at the busy street, watching for customers and occasionally calling in his soft, courteous voice to shoppers who stop to peer into the display windows. He is a short, handsome young man, with the thick black hair and warmly dark skin and eyes of an East Indian. In many ways, he seems as foreign in the British atmosphere and among the British soldiers and sailors as the incense-burning statues and the carved elephant tusks he sells—but Gibraltar is his home.

Although he is just twenty, Krishna is already a man of many countries. As a resident of Gibraltar, the first child of

Indian parents born on the rock, he is a British subject. He has lived in France and was educated in Tangier and Gibraltar. On a clear day, he can stand on the beaches of Gibraltar and look over to Africa. Any Sunday afternoon, he can take a bus ride over the one-mile peninsula that joins the big rock to Spain—see a bullfight, eat paella (the rice and chicken dish of Spain), or watch gypsy dancing. He can speak English, Spanish, French and a little German. He, like many of his relatives, has migrated to a strange land in his career as a merchant; others in his family have settled in such scattered areas as Tangier, Singapore and Nairobi, on the east Coast of Africa. But for Krishna, happiest memories still live in India, many hundreds of miles away. He can watch the busy, cosmopolitan streets of Gibraltar—and dream of the trip that will someday take him back to India, to find himself a wife.

At one time Krishna was one of seven children. He was born on Gibraltar, just five months after his mother and father made the long trip from Hyderabad, India. There were only three Indian families on Gibraltar then (there are now fourteen) and Krishna's grandfather ran a small shop, to sell silks, ivories and curiosities to visitors. Gibraltar is always so crowded with troops, barracks and defense areas, mostly closed to the non-military public, that the small space left for the 23,000 permanent residents of the big rock is limited and cramped, but Krishna and his family were comfortable and well off.

Then came 1940, when the little boy with the big, dark eyes was just five years old. The British needed every bit of space—and security—they could get on The Rock for the 43,000 troops housed there during World War II, and

[77]

Krishna and his family, except for an older brother, began the long evacuation trek to India. It was a sad journey for the little boy.

"We were all on the same ship," he says, his eyes still pained from the memories. "My mother and father, my two brothers, three sisters and I. We had already passed down around Capetown in Africa and were just about two days from India when our ship was captured by a German raider. The Germans took us all on board as prisoners and then sank our ship.

"For three weeks we stayed on the German raider and sailed toward France. The raider sank four other Allied ships while we were on board. Finally, we were all transferred to a Norwegian ship the Germans had captured. But this ship flew a German flag and, just a few miles off the coast of France, we were torpedoed by a British submarine." Even though the tragedy was sixteen years in the past, the memory brought a look of fear to Krishna's face.

"I was just a little boy but the instinct for self-preservation made me move very fast. As the ship tipped, I ran to a top deck and hung on to a railing. Another Indian, an old man who had worked as our cook in Gibraltar, saw me and helped me onto a raft. Then the ship sank. I lost my whole family who were aboard in one hour. After that torpedo hit, I never saw them again."

About four hours later, the survivors on the raft, including Krishna, were picked up by a French ship. But the German army was already occupying France and, since a small boy wasn't wanted in a prison camp, he was simply left with an Indian family stranded in Rouen, France. ("The woman was having a baby and the Germans didn't want her, either,"

[78]

Krishna explained.) After a year in France, relatives arranged for the young boy to be sent to the city of Tangier, in a then international zone in Africa, right across from Gibraltar. Here he and the older brother who had remained behind when the family left Gibraltar went to school with the Christian Brothers until the end of the war. By 1945, with the war over, Krishna went back to Gibraltar, to live with an uncle and finish his high school education.

"Those were nice years," says Krishna. "School until four o'clock, then tea at home and then out with my friends—day after day the same." Even though Gibraltar is only three miles long and three-quarters of a mile wide, with a total area of two and a quarter miles, Krishna and his friends found room to have fun. He joined the Sea Scouts, became a Cub Master in the Boy Scouts, played field hockey and, in his last year in school, won the class swimming championship. At sixteen, he had had all the formal education to be found on Gibraltar and life suddenly became a serious problem.

"I decided to go to India," he explained, "to be with my maternal grandmother. I had always been lonesome for more family and I felt I would be happy there. My grandmother was kind to me, I had many cousins and for the first time since I was a little boy, I felt I was with people who loved me.

"It was then that I became ambitious to do something in life. I began to study very hard. At the University of Lucknow, I studied chemistry, biology, botany and zoology and got my Bachelor of Science degree. Then I tried to take the premedical exams because I had decided I wanted to be a doctor. But somehow I could not get the necessary permit

[79]

—I was not an Indian citizen, I was not a refugee from Pakistan—I was nothing.

"So there was nothing for me to do but travel. I went through India, from Bombay to Darjeeling and then New Delhi—then to Rangoon and Singapore. But my relatives kept writing to me to remind me that I was coming of age and must claim my inheritance. I had responsibilities. My father had left me this store. So I came back to Gibraltar and now I am a merchant."

He looked about the store, cool and dark after the glare of the street. The shelves were piled neatly with rolls of silk, cashmere sweaters and rows of expensive perfumes. Three clerks stood close at the elbows of shoppers who were looking into the showcase of special Indian merchandise. Near Krishna's desk, at the back of the shop, was a table from which he might serve a glass of cognac, with a cigarette or a cup of strong black coffee, to favored customers, an old and gracious custom with Indian shopkeepers. (However, Indians of the Moslem faith never touch alcoholic drinks.) Everything in Krishna's store was in perfect order. "Perhaps this is the better life," he said quietly. "Perhaps I would not have been a *good* doctor. . . ."

And what *is* life like for a young Indian merchant in Gibraltar? For Krishna it is mostly hard work—and dreaming. He works six days a week, from nine in the morning to nine-thirty at night, with two hours off for lunch (usually an exotic Indian curry dish) at the home of his uncle, with whom he still lives. (Following the custom of neighboring Spain, all the shops on Gibraltar are shut for three hours at midday.) At least two nights a week, Krishna goes to the movies; most of the time he simply goes home to read himself to sleep. (In the movies, he prefers Jennifer Jones above all because she is "so real and so simple.") Gibraltar has a number of bars and cafes, some open to the street, where small jazz bands entertain the customers after five in the afternoon, but Krishna has no time for this. Occasionally, on Sundays, he may go swimming at Catalan Bay, a tiny fishing village on the eastern side of the rock. The town, just a scattering of homes and shops on a half moon of beach, can be reached only through a stretch of the thirty miles of tunneling that the British have bored through the sturdy rock of Gibraltar. The tunnels contain not only ammunitions, fortifications and fuel supplies but also—during World War II—they housed complete hospital facilities. The little village of Catalan Bay was founded years ago, when Genoese fishermen were washed by a storm onto this isolated shore. Their descendants are still the chief residents of the town.

But for Krishna most of life is the life of his shop, long hours and hard, demanding work—because for him the most important part of his existence still lies ahead and he is determined to be ready for it.

When he talked about his plans for the future, his voice was warm, without shyness. "I put aside a certain sum of money each month. In a few years, when I am about twenty-five, I will be ready to go back to India to find a wife.

"In India, my family still does things by the old customs. For instance, when I was with my grandmother last time, I received three proposals of marriage. According to our custom, the families of three marriageable girls sent notes to my grandmother, asking to talk over marriage possibilities. She wrote back to thank them and to say that I was still too busy with my studies for marriage."

[81]

When he does make the great "bride trip" back to India, Krishna thinks it should take him no more than three to six months to decide on the girl he wants as a wife—and to marry her. "My relatives will give little parties. I will have a chance to see girls of whom they approve—and the girls will have a chance to see me. Before the families make formal marriage proposals, we would both know all about each other. Her family will discuss everything among themselves —what I am like, my business, do I drink or smoke—even such things as whether or not I wear glasses." (He neither smokes nor wears glasses, but does take a drink occasionally with Gibraltar friends. However, he does not expect to drink while in India because he would not want to offend the family of his bride-to-be, who might be Moslem.)

Though he has many friends, both English and Spanish, Krishna is definite about wanting an Indian girl as his wife. "We would understand each other," he explains simply. And for the girl, he has already made firm plans.

"She will probably be about eighteen or nineteen, because that is the age at which girls of my class usually marry. And she will have to speak English, since I know almost no Indian dialects after my years here. Perhaps in the begin- ning we will have to take just a room or two here in Gibraltar. Later I would like to build a home over the border, in Spain. We would like the life there—it is full of leisure, the land is beautiful and living is cheap. (Gibraltar belonged to the Spaniards at one time but was captured by the British about two hundred and fifty years ago. Though British travelers are free to go into Spain on a visa and about fourteen thousand Spaniards come and go into Gibraltar to work each day, there is still a cool feeling between the two countries over ownership of the great rock.)

"By the time I marry, I will have my own car," said Krishna. "I could drive to my shop in the morning. Then sometimes, in the late afternoon, I would send one of my clerks back for my wife. We would spend an evening here with my friends—go out for dinner and to the movies. Sometimes on Saturdays there are tea dances at one of the hotels. I would like my wife to dance here even if it wasn't her custom in India. Later, when we have children, I will drive them here to school in the morning. . . .

"I want my wife to have freedom," he explained carefully, his face suddenly intense and possessive. "But she must care for the house, give orders to the servants and take good care of the children. I would like her to be nice to my friends, be able to talk with them—but she must never be too friendly. I think I would be very jealous."

Reserved and courteous in manner, warmly handsome in appearance, Krishna Khubchand is, underneath, a clear-thinking, very determined young man. He has never quite joined the English world of Gibraltar, he will never quite leave India behind. By marrying an Indian bride, he will always have a part of the land of his parents close by him. Then, even with India thousands of miles away, he will feel once again that he is "with people who really love me."

5

BRIGITTE ZAHN

West Berlin, Germany

THE LAST TIME I saw Brigitte Zahn, she was standing on
a West Berlin street corner, waving good-bye after my
taxi. That was five years ago, when she was nineteen. It was
a bitterly cold night but with great courtesy she stood waving
and smiling while the wind whipped her red wool scarf and
a thin snow settled over the crumbled war ruins behind her.
This is Brigitte's story as I wrote it then.

Except for the three years at the end of the war, when she fled to the country to escape Allied bombing, Brigitte Zahn has always lived in Berlin. "Sometimes Berliners say, 'We are prisoners of the city we love,'" says Brigitte, a gangling, fresh-faced beauty of nineteen. "But I am a city girl. I like the excitement. A little country house is good for week ends, but I would be bored if I had to live away from Berlin."

Brigitte lives now with her parents and an older sister and brother in a sprawling six-room apartment in the British Sector of the city, not far from Tempelhof Airfield. The building, which houses nineteen other families, was given to Mrs. Zahn by her father on her wedding day, thirty-two years ago. It still has traces of elegance—stained glass trim on the windows, fat cement balconies and curtained French doors—but the building, like the rest of the street and the people who live on it, has lost most of its prosperity since the war. On the corner stand the ravished and burned-out ruins of the former Nazi Air Ministry. Just two doors from the Zahn apartment, a lot lies empty, picked clean by city rubble workers of the bricks and debris left by a direct hit during the war. Many of the buildings are pocked with bomb fragments; here and there you will see a splintered door crudely repaired with new wood, a broken window bricked in against the weather.

But to Brigitte all these war scars have long since become part of the street scenery and she barely sees them as she rushes to catch a seven-fifteen street car for school each morning. Even after a half-hour ride, there is still a brisk four-block walk to make her eight-o'clock class in the battered old building of the Kreuzberg Higher School for Girls. Though she points out firmly that "everyone knows I am no lazybones," Brigitte is a little older than most of the twelve other girls in her class. Like many other German students, she lost two years of schooling during the war, first when she was evacuated with her sister, Inge, to a youth camp in Upper Silesia, and later when she worked as a farm hand in Bavaria and as a maid in Bamberg.

"To be evacuated was our 'voluntary duty,'" explained Brigitte. "We were seventeen in all—two teachers, my classmates, my sister and I. I was just twelve, so I took my Johann with me (a fuzzy white teddy bear, a gift on her eighth birthday). He was a very brave beast," she said fondly. "He fled with me everywhere and then right back to my bedroom."

Both Zahn girls began the evacuation trip hopefully— Brigitte took three suitcases of clothing and, the first winter, even wrote home for her feather bed. Soon, however, the disaster became clear to them, first in terms of loneliness, then in hunger and finally in fear. They did not see their parents again for over three years (their only brother, Hans, was taken prisoner of war with an antiaircraft unit in Africa, early in 1940, and was not returned to Berlin until 1946) and it was not until six years and ten months after Brigitte packed that first suitcase that the Zahn family again lived together under one roof.

Mrs. Zahn, a warm, pretty woman in her early fifties, from whom Brigitte inherits both a twinkling eye and a lightness of spirit, commented with a concern she never lets her daughters see, "Both girls are still changed a little. When they came home, they were too quiet, too old. Brigitte is more like herself again. But Inge is more reserved, more silent than she was as a little girl."

Though she was always too young to be considered a voting part of the Hitler regime, Brigitte's relationship with the Third Reich was not completely impersonal. In 1942, at the age of ten, she did become a member of the Hitler Youth Group (membership became mandatory in 1939). And she does remember seeing Adolf Hitler for the first time in 1936, as a five-year-old child, when he drove around th Olympia Stadium in Berlin, in an open car, during the Olympic Games. She saw him again several times before she fled the city in 1943 and admits candidly, "I thought Hitler was one of the most handsome men I ever saw." With equal candor, and with the curious confidence of many young Germans whose ideas have changed more by circumstances than by conviction, Brigitte says even now, "I was very disappointed that we lost the war. I was very young and had been told so many good things would happen if we won."

Brigitte's initial child-sized taste of defeat began in the Silesian youth camp. For the first year and three months, she and Inge, just three years her senior, had been living in community life with other children, keeping up with their schooling. However, as Russian troops neared, the group was transferred to a camp in Czechoslovakia. A few months later, as Allied troops pressed farther into German territory, the children fled 180 miles, first on foot, then by truck, to the safety of the farm lands of Bavaria. At one point, the fighting was so close that a bullet hit Inge's suitcase and exploded it open at her feet.

In Bavaria, the group found shelter in a deserted Nazi work camp and went out to beg work from local farmers. Brigitte found a job cleaning stables and laboring in the fields, turning hay to dry from seven in the morning till nine

[87]

at night. Characteristically, with her "things aren't *so* bad" attitude, she commented, "I was lucky. Most of the city girls knew nothing about farms and were very unhappy. But I had handled sheep and things at our week-end house in the country and I knew all about it."

Both Zahn girls were still working as farm hands when the war ended in 1945. Of that period Brigitte tells a small but revealing anecdote about herself which might indicate either a young and healthy confidence in people—or her own lack of feeling of involvment with the conflict. One day, when she was feeding a young calf, it broke its tether and went skittering off through the barn, the feed bucket caught on its head. A Polish girl, watching, laughed at Brigitte but refused to help her. "It was so silly of her to feel that way just because I was a German," says Brigitte with some heat. "The calf might have broken his leg!"

A few months later, Brigitte was transferred to Bamberg, to earn her room and board as a "house daughter," or maid, in a church institution. Brother Hans, after spending four years as a prisoner of war in Tennessee and in Virginia, had been transferred to England. The older Zahns, fleeing from occupied Berlin, took refuge at their former week-end house, a thatch-roofed farmhouse on three acres, about fifty miles from the city. Suddenly fifteen-year-old Brigitte, reacting to the tension of the war years, became "ill with homesickness" and wrote pleading letters to her family about coming home. After several weeks of maneuvering, an aunt managed to get her transportation back to Berlin, to an apartment just a few blocks from her present school. "She is my favorite aunt and was very kind to me," explains Brigitte, who has a strong family feeling. "And I was glad to be with her then.

My uncle had just been taken off by the Russians. He was not a Nazi, but in those days Germans were all denouncing Germans, and we think someone just wanted to get even. We think he must be dead."

Abruptly, after more than three hectic, deeply disturbing years, Brigitte tried to return to the ordinary life of a schoolgirl. Her father, now working in a sawmill, sent her five dollars a month, to buy clothes and take care of school expenses; during occasional visits to her parents in the country, Mr. Zahn helped Brigitte with her French and "tutored her in Latin until she cried." (Though he has always been in the real estate business, Fritz Zahn is a graduate of The Cloisters and speaks French as well as German. His wife speaks a little English as well.) Hans was released from prison camp and came back to live in one room of the family apartment in Berlin. With Inge now studying nursing, life began to settle down to an irregular but somewhat permanent postwar pattern.

But for Brigitte, the transition back to peace was not easy. In what she soberly calls "the horrible winters" (1947 and 1948), when other Berliners cut down the trees in the city parks and tried to pull bits of wood out of the midtown debris for fuel, Brigitte often visited her parents' farm, to drag back fifty-pound sacks of kindling for the stove in her aunt's apartment. But one day the temperature in her bedroom dropped to six below zero. Brigitte caught influenza. A few days later, it developed into pneumonia and she went to the hospital for four weeks. "I was studying so hard," she explained, "that I felt I had no time to lie down. Then suddenly I am ill for good. In the hospital, I was almost more sick than ever because the food was so bad. I just couldn't make myself eat dried mashed potatoes all the time." Later that year, partly from strain and partly from many months of scanty diet, Brigitte developed stomach ulcers so severe that she often had to leave school during the day to go home to rest. Then came an accident that brought her nearer to despair than anything that happened during the war years. During gymnasium period in the school court-yard, she slipped and broke her ankle. Even now she cannot talk about it lightly. "There was nothing to do then but ask the teacher if I might be allowed to take the year over."

But in a city like Berlin, Brigitte's troubles were not unique. Most of her classmates, equally juggled about by the war, have faced similar physical and emotional difficulties in reaching their last year of school. The Kreuzberg senior class, thirteen girls ranging in age from sixteen to twenty-one, sit like a cross section of the disruption and personal tragedy typical of all German youth since the war. The oldest student is a twenty-one-year-old Polish Jew who spent most of her teen years in a concentration camp. One classmate "holds the record," as she puts it, by having been bombed out of her Berlin home three times. Another is a member of the *Freie Deutsche Jugend* (Free German Youth), one of the 1000 Free German Youth members, the very active Communist youth group, living in West Berlin. In direct contrast is a fellow student so anti-Communist that she defies the East Sector law to come to school each morning from her home in that section of the city. Just a few months ago, this student was expelled from her East Sector school and forbidden to attend school at all for writing a strong essay against the Free German Youth rally, which brought 500,000 blue-shirted members of that group marching from all East Germany into Berlin last spring. ("Is it possible," she wrote, "that after all that has happened in the Nazi times, youth again should be deceived by the waving of flags, by marching and hailing? Many people will still remember that it started in 1933 quite similarly.")

But in spite of the mixed enrollment, the atmosphere in the classroom is unusually intense and congenial, with the students, all poor and shabbily dressed, working and reciting as if they were determined to make up for lost time. Even Brigitte looks a little too large, a little too mature to be crowded into the small desk. "My classmates are all good comrades," she insists vigorously. "We have no arguments at all unless we talk politics."

At the Kreuzberg school, cramped and in need of new equipment, as are most of the Berlin schools, the students stay in the same classroom all day long (except for science and art periods) and the teachers change about. Even Director Frederick Kranendick, an elderly bachelor and a great favorite with the students, doubles as a math teacher. Between classes, Brigitte—who was elected to the office for the year—hurries to wipe the two small blackboards or roll up the maps, while the others talk at their desks, do some last-minute cramming or rush to comb their hair at an improvised mirror, made by opening a small window inward so it catches the dark reflection of the blackboard. (The school has no washrooms in the main building. However, a small, cement-floored structure, about twenty yards away, is fitted with half-a-dozen toilets, but no washbasin, towels or mirrors.)

All the students in Brigitte's class take the same required curriculum: four languages, mathematics, chemistry, geography, biology, history, music, art appreciation and gymnastics, with two hours of religion a week optional. (Brigitte attends a Protestant church on special holidays, but feels too busy to fit religion into her school schedule this year.) Twice a week, after her last class, she goes to an ex-schoolteacher for tutoring in English and French.

The most exciting event of the week takes place every Friday, when the class is turned into a free-for-all forum for an hour, with no teacher present. The day Brigitte was chairman, the subject for discussion was: "Are careers for women a good thing or a necessary evil?" (Previous discussions, all suggested by the students, covered such problems as mercy killing, corrective legislation for insane asylums and the question, "Should women have a place in politics?") As Brigitte pounded on the teacher's desk with the lid of a lunch pail, to keep order, the girls exchanged, and shouted, such opinions as "Professional women can't have two careers at once—therefore they must make a choice between home and job!" . . . "There are statistics to show that women *do not have* the same intellectual capacity as men!" and "Shame on you! You condemn yourselves to the stove!" The student from the Free German Youth group got no argument from the class with her statement that "Work should be a joy—a woman should be allowed to be a brickmason if it makes her happy." Brigitte herself, pink-cheeked with authority, wound up the discussion by stating that, "I think it is the natural calling of a woman to make a home and have children. It is mean to call us slaves!"

Each day at Kreuzberg, as at every other public school in Berlin, the class schedule is interrupted for the "school feeding," a free hot lunch which supplements student diet by

350 calories. Prepared in city kitchens, the food is delivered to the schools in insulated cans, and promptly at ten-thirty, class monitors scoop out into enameled pails enough food to supply their classrooms. The menu is varied regularly, with thick stews, soups, rice puddings and, one day a week, cocoa with raisin buns. Last fall, when some students got too finicky about the food, Director Kranendick cut the daily order by fifty portions, but most girls scrape their bowls to the bottom.

To support the school feeding in West Berlin schools, the United States Government contributes about $2,125,000 a year, the city government about $1,225,000, with the French and British governments also contributing liberally. "School feeding" is also a part of the program in the Soviet-controlled sector of the city but the menus there are less appealing than those of the West Sector, consisting chiefly of cereals, sauerkraut soup with black bread and a kind of soupy pudding made from the residue of flax after it has been pressed for oil.

At Kreuzberg, no student is allowed to leave the grounds during the school hours—from eight o'clock to one-thirty each day, six days a week—but after each feeding period, the girls are allowed fifteen minutes for promenading around the big walled-in school courtyard. Over that red brick wall, if no teacher is nearby, the girls can wave to students looking out of the windows of the boys' school just a few doors away. For the younger girls, these promenades are just giggling interludes. For the older girls, they sometimes serve as a way to get acquainted with boys and to arrange walk-home meetings for after school. Even though the two schools exchange invitations to gym dances twice a year, friendship is strictly discouraged between times.

[93]

"It's so silly," says Brigitte, "because we all know one another. All but two of the girls in my class have special friends—and we do have our little balls together!" These "little balls," financed by the students and given at Christmas or graduation time, are held from six to nine, in the school gym, with a small orchestra and teachers from both schools as chaperons. "For each ball, we all give a little money—I have more than some, so I give about fifteen cents," Brigitte explained.

It was at such an after-school dance that Brigitte met both of the boys who have so far been important in her life. The first friendship ended with some sadness a couple of summers ago, when the boy went to West Germany to work during the vacation—and didn't write. "In all that time, I got only two post cards, so I put him behind the mirror," said Brigitte blithely, using one of the few slang phrases in the German teen-ager's vocabulary. ("To put behind the mirror" means simply "to forget." A handsome boy or a girl might be referred to as "a cloud," to fall in love is "to bang" and teen-aged girls themselves are known as *backfisch,* the little fish too small to be considered a legitimate catch.)

The second and most important friendship is with an exceedingly handsome boy, now a twenty-one-year-old chemistry student from Bonn University. ("My aunt says he is so handsome he looks like a girl," Brigitte explained proudly.) Though she admits that, "I sometimes have little rendezvous I don't even tell my mother about," her current boy is the first one to get full family approval, since the Zahns did not allow their daughter to invite boys to the apartment till her nineteenth birthday. But now Brigitte keeps his picture in the bedroom she shares with Inge, and when he was home for eight days last Christmas, she saw him every day, invited him to the family New Year's party and went with him to several plays and concerts. "And we always managed just to catch the last trolley home at twelve-thirty!" she added.

Partly because it is German tradition and partly because the Zahns are unabashedly grateful to be together again, most of Brigitte's life outside school is spent at home and with her family. The big apartment is also used as an office, from which father and son conduct their real estate business. With Mr. Zahn, portly and impressive in dark coat, gray striped trousers and spats, always on hand for clients, the Zahn household has a dressed-up, ready-for-business air about it. The front room is filled with worn red plush furniture, with plump cushions embroidered by Brigitte and her mother. Strips of mellowed Persian carpet cover the floor, and on one wall hangs a large original oil painting of a drinking scene from *The Student Prince*. In the middle of the room, in front of the bay windows, are Mr. Zahn's massive carved desk and chair.

In the "old days," as the Zahns refer to the prewar period, the family were very well off, with a car, the week-end house in the country and vacations at the East Sea. Now the country house is inaccessible, for it is in the Russian Zone. Two of the five Zahn apartment buildings were bombed out in the war, and a third, recently condemned as unsafe, would need $20,000 to put it in repair. Though both Hans and Mr. Zahn are kept busy managing their property, as well as negotiating wills and handling mortgages for others, Brigitte says she "just has to beg" her father for the $2.50 a month she gets as an allowance, two dollars of which goes for a transportation ticket to get to school.

Nevertheless, the Fritz Zahn house has a feeling of warmth and near affluence about it, and Mr. Zahn is a sentimentally affectionate father. Inge, less outgoing in her personality than Brigitte, often slips over to hug him from behind as he sits in his big chair, while Brigitte is more casually and adolescently disrespectful in her affection.

At the end of the war, six families lived jammed in the Zahn apartment, one family to a room. Now, though no painting or papering has been done for ten years, the windows shattered by bomb blasts have been replaced, there is coal for the stoves in every room and Mrs. Zahn never misses baking "the Sunday cake," usually a marble cake or a hazelnut cake with whipped cream. Brigitte has learned how to cook from her mother, and, though her heavy homework schedule sometimes limits her kitchen help to squeezing whipped-cream designs on the baking, she is especially good at making doughnuts and a rich goulash of beef, tomatoes, onions and seasoning.

Tall and with a bouncy energy, Brigitte translates her weight from kilos into about 124 pounds and never worries about dieting. Though she often tries to skip the roll and hot tea her mother prepares for her breakfast, she is hungry at almost every other hour of the day. Amusingly, however, she is completely unaware of her big appetite. "Sometimes," she explained naively, "when I'm not hungry, I eat two slices of pumpernickel bread and that helps." Even her family, used to rich, heavy food, teases her about the whipped cream she heaps on her Sunday cake. "But I didn't have any from

1938 till eleven years later," she says, "and I just can't get enough."

It is perhaps at family parties that Mrs. Zahn's cooking and Brigitte's appetite show at their peak. Cakes with whipped cream and coffee are the usual refreshments, with occasional beer and brandy for the men, sherry for the women. Saturday night is always best for such gatherings, or a birthday or New Year's Eve. The guests are close relatives—aunts, uncles, cousins, some as young as three years old—and the Zahn family. After refreshments, most of the evening is spent in dancing. With her cousins, Brigitte likes to tango or do a kind of wide, sweeping jitterbug. A radio and a phonograph stand in one corner of the dining room, and, by pushing back the table, the dancers can swing around the parquet floor until the cut glass on the sideboard jingles. There is a grand piano in the living room, and, though Brigitte, who took lessons in more prosperous times, no longer plays, her mother can accompany as both sing *Suwannee River* and other Southern songs in English for their guests. (Hans became especially fond of Southern music during his stay as a prisoner of war in the United States, so last Christmas Brigitte gave him a favorite recording, in German, of *Carry Me Back to Old Virginny*.)

"Our parties at home are so good," explained Brigitte with enthusiasm, "that my classmates sometimes get envious when I tell about them!"

For Brigitte, most parties away from home are also family affairs. It was with her parents that she went out for her only two "long nights" (dancing till dawn) and this year she got her first formal dress, a peach-colored silk with ruching around the scoop neckline, for a dance given by her father's all-male social club. This dress, like most of the things in her wardrobe, Brigitte designed herself, then had made by a neighborhood tailor. "I am not ashamed," she says, "that my wardrobe is so small. I am building it up little by little." But to many girls, Brigitte's wardrobe would seem adequate; to many Berliners, almost lavish. In her closet are three skirts, five blouses, two sweaters, four summer dresses, two wool dresses and a heavy wool coat. Each dress, including material and sewing, cost about eleven dollars. "Sometimes," Brigitte said, "Inge and I change around to make things go farther. I like pretty clothes, but I am also happy without them because, by nature, I have a light spirit."

But Brigitte's "light spirit," as well as the peace of mind of the rest of the Zahn family, is sometimes overshadowed by two things: first, the difficulty of keeping economically stable in a city still far from recovered from the war; and second, making daily and future plans with the knowledge that Berlin as a city, and they as a people, are surrounded on all sides by Russian-controlled territory, a full 120 miles from the nearest Allied zone. Economically, the Zahns have reached a kind of bearable status quo; the Russians, or at least the group antipathy for them, has been adopted almost as a family hobby.

The Zahns are quick to blame every material loss they have suffered on the Russians. Their summer home happened to lie in a territory declared Russian by the Potsdam agreement, but during the first days after the war, Mrs. Zahn's beaver coat and a quantity of crystal and silver were looted from the apartment. These losses, as well as furniture damage, nicked picture frames or broken windows, are attributed to the Soviet troops. However, the Zahns' actual contact with the Russians has been close enough and frightening enough to warrant their apprehension.

After the elder Zahns went to live at their country house in 1945, it took them five years to get permission from the Russian authorities to come back to West Berlin. In the meantime, just after the end of hostilities, Mr. Zahn was arrested by the Russians. With eleven other men from the small village near his farm, he was kept prisoner for two weeks.

"They thought my father must have been an army officer," says Brigitte, "because he was so fine and tall and had such smooth hands." After two weeks, Mr. Zahn and one other man were released.

Even Brigitte, who has never even seen a Russian soldier in Berlin, has absorbed fear from the experiences of her family, as well as from what she has heard about the Russians and conditions in their zone. "I don't even like to listen to the music on their radio stations," she said, "because then you have to hear all the speeches and talk about Stalin." Only on the rarest occasions does she make a trip into the Eastern Sector of the city, and then it is with a precaution that might fit into an old-fashioned spy story. For instance, last January Brigitte and her classmates all went over for a performance of *Faust* as part of their German course. The old Berlin Opera House is in the East Sector and even the Westerners admit that the best opera is still there. "But we didn't go together," Brigitte explained. "We each went over alone, by elevated train, and though I sat next to one of my comrades, the others were all scattered around. No one from this sector likes to be seen over there as a crowd."

It is through omnipresent propaganda that the Russians

have stamped their claim on the East Sector of the city. The fluttering flags and Communist posters are everywhere. Swung across several main streets, giant red banners read, "It is only the friendship between Germany and Russia that keeps the United States from bringing war to our soil!" Currently, the most popular poster, plastered on walls by the thousands, is a picture of a woeful small boy's face, one large tear about to fall, with the caption, "For the sake of our children—Ami, go home!"

Last spring, when East Berlin played host to half a million members of the Free German Youth, Brigitte's brother saw a seventeen-year-old boy, in the blue uniform shirt of the Communist youth group, wandering disconsolately down the famous Kurfurstendamm, in the West Sector. "Hansi asked the boy to come for lunch with us," explains Brigitte. "He was very nice—told us he was a forestry apprentice from Thuringia and that he'd been forced to come to the rally or lose his job. He even had to buy shoes for the trip. He stayed first for lunch, then for coffee and then supper. My father gave him a little money to buy presents for his little sister and, after dark, Hans took him to a street where he could slip into the East Sector without being seen. We told him not to write to us because it might be dangerous for him."

Though Brigitte's contacts with the American Occupation are more friendly than those with the Russians, they are equally casual and infrequent. American magazines and newspapers are used in her English class, when the students can get them, but Brigitte had never actually talked to an American. "None of my friends would date American soldiers," she said simply. "Neither would I. You know why.

We have no way to be introduced to them and it would be terrible just to be picked up on the street."

For the future of Germany, Brigitte has no solution at all, but rather one firm conviction: "We cannot stay split, Germans against Germans. We want to be free. If we are helped, we can be free again. Alone, we are not strong enough, but some day Germany will stand by herself."

About her own immediate future she is less concerned and more confident, making plans within the shell of danger, as if her fate were completely in her own hands. On first question, Brigitte always answers enthusiastically, "I want to be a food chemist. I am thinking of going to the Free University of Berlin. But," she must then add, "the Free University is already filled for the next two years, though I hear they may open a new chemistry building next year." Then, faced with the realization that she will be graduated from the Kreuzberg school by the end of June, the future suddenly becomes close and demanding. Having survived a rugged past, Brigitte can also realistically face a rugged future.

"I think what I will try to do is find a job, if I can, as an apothecary's assistant. That will be a two-year apprenticeship in some shop nearby. When I finish, I earn $12.50 a week and have a limited license to practice. In the meantime, I get about eight dollars a month—enough for me if I live at home."

But even that two-year apprenticeship may be cut short for a more permanent working arrangement, because Brigitte admits with frank enthusiasm, "I think marriage is a good idea—and the sooner the better!" And for Brigitte, there will be no conflicting choice between a career and marriage.

"I think women are just made for marriage and I like to take care of a house. I want to have many children—four, I think. I want them to have a free life, but they must learn to obey me and not be naughty. No crying, no bad words in my house. Some day I would even like to have my own week-end house in the country.

"You know," she added disarmingly, remembering even as she spoke that the countryside around Berlin no longer belonged either to her or to the city itself, "I am a very gay person. I could dance all night without two coins in my pocket!"

And in today's mail, in Brigitte's small, neat handwriting, comes a letter with this sequel to her story:

"Some dreams came true and some didn't. After high school I didn't have the money to get into college. So for two years I worked in a big dress store on our main avenue, Kurfurstendamm. I was able to save, yet buy myself many things—shoes, blouses and a warm coat. And one summer I went with many friends on a camping trip into Italy and Switzerland.

"The third year I took a business course and quickly learned typing and shorthand. And then my childhood dream (my wildest) began to come true. I started studying medicine at the Free University of Berlin. I am now in my third year and, though it is very hard and the hours long, I love it. And I know I will finish the course.

"Both my brother and sister are married and my parents are well, though older. Mother still has her old hobby: baking fat apple-cakes. My handsome boy friend from the University of Bonn? He disappeared from my life without a word! But I don't mind. I have another boy friend and many girl friends and when I finish my education—I will have time for love.

"Since your visit, we have many new buildings, parks and streets. West Berlin has a new dress but East Berlin is still a dark, sad place. In most other ways, life is the same but happier than ever. Now, except for studies, I have nothing to worry about at all. . . ."

6

PETUR SNAELAND

Iceland

O N THE WORLD MAP, Iceland seems little more than a jagged inkblot floating high in the cold North Atlantic. On closer look, it is a small but fascinating country of mix-ups, an island about which nature has not yet made up its mind.

Just 40,000 square miles in all, Iceland is a combination of flat grasslands that melt off into the horizon, rugged, untracked mountain wastes, chasmed, rumbling glaciers and live, smoking volcanoes—plus neat, prosperous towns, a-hum with radios and taxicabs.

There are hundreds of birds, yet almost no insects, and not a single frog, snake or other reptile on the island. Inland lakes jump with trout, but, except for a few foxes (and seals swimming in the coves), the land has no wild animals. In some areas, acres of summertime flowers fill the air with fragrance; yet in the center of the island, ageless glaciers stretch for miles, barren and majestic, defying human habitation. An April blizzard may sweep blindingly across flat plains with fissures in the earth huff up breaths of steam, right through the snow.

Icelanders speak a language dating back to the 800's A.D., but not a building on the island is over fifty years old. There is not a mile of railroad, not a single navigable river but the country averages one car per thirteen people and every Icelander must learn to swim before he can leave school. Windswept, isolated and remote, nature dropped this island in an ocean path almost halfway between Russia and the United States. (2,800 miles from Washington, 2,000 miles from Moscow.) Its nearest neighbor, backward, icebound Greenland, is over 200 miles away. And to illuminate this strange climatic and geographic stirabout, so close to the North Pole, so far from the rest of the world, a bright "midnight sun" sometimes shines down for twenty-four hours a day.

Petur Snaeland has lived in Iceland for seventeen years, since the day he was born in the neat brown house on Tringata Street. Petur's home is in Reykjavik, the capital city of the island, and he knows every street, every pastel house, every snow-capped mountain rimming the horizon by heart.

Down near the harbor, whipped endlessly by the ocean winds, is his father's rubber factory, a tall, boxlike building with the hasty, makeshift look so typical of Iceland's architecture. A few blocks away, sitting on the shores of a trim artificial lake, is one of the local theaters, painted a gay minty green, where dramatic companies put on plays such as *Death of a Salesman* and *Life with Father*. Up two blocks on a slanting street stands the Hotel Borg, brown and somber, with room for forty-five guests and tea dances on Sunday. Here the King of Denmark, state head of Iceland till 1944, comes on his diplomatic visits. Off the main square of the town, is the *menntaskoli*, where Petur is in his third year. It is fronted by broad stone steps, like many big-city high schools.

Reykjavik, the glamour city of the island, has the air of a Yukon boom town. Streets are crowded with cars and well-dressed shoppers; store windows are jammed with the newest stoves, refrigerators and washing machines, clothing and record players and even such unsuspected luxuries as stuffed olives, nylon sweaters and harmonicas. There are spired churches, a good museum and the huge dark-stone National Theater, as well as seven small movie theaters with bright posters plastered round the door. And there is a bus station where heavy buses, road-weary and crowded, leave every hour for surrounding country towns. At the docks, swooping with sea gulls, occasional immaculate white passenger ships, usually commuters from Scotland, tie up among the neat fishing trawlers and the cargo vessels that supply Iceland with goods from all over the world.

There are over 60,000 people in Reykjavik and it bustles with activity, yet it is like a small town. And like any small town teen-ager, restless and with time on his hands (plus the family car when he wants it), Petur Snaeland knows every square block.

He is the oldest of three boys, and the two youngest brothers—round-faced teasers in overalls and plaid shirts—seem "the children" in the family, with Petur ranking as adult with his parents. Slight, not very tall and a little serious behind his glasses, Petur is an excellent student, alert and confident, though still a bit too shy to make use of his good sense of humor and perceptive wit. "I don't mean to say that I'm speaking for all the boys in our school," he said defensively, "but I don't go out with girls myself. Not yet, that is."

Right now, Petur is somewhat overshadowed by his energetic, good-looking parents. His mother, a former commercial artist, is a bright-eyed, pretty woman who speaks English like a New Yorker and in her own teens worked as a guide for English-speaking tourists. Mr. Snaeland towers above his son. A brisk, prosperous businessman, he operated a garage until it burned down four years ago. Now his new factory imports rubber milk from Malaya and air-whips it into foam rubber for use on the island. Next project for Mr. Snaeland: a factory for making ready-to-assemble furniture for Icelanders. He owns his own plane, one of thirty private planes on the island, and likes to fly to the northern areas occasionally for trout fishing with friends.

The brown house on Tringata Street is full of old-fashioned, homey comfort. Two-storied, with a wide side porch, it is warm, well-carpeted and full of furniture that shows the wear and tear of three boys. The living room is shelved with books (there is not a single illiterate in all of Iceland and even the tiniest hamlet has a public library), the walls are bright with pictures. Icelanders are home-proud people and though weather may make the outdoors bleak and gray, the houses are snug and full of color. Oil paintings are popular gifts to newlyweds, and at a recent show in Reykjavik, sixteen canvases sold the first day, some bringing as high as fifteen hundred dollars.

Petur is a hungry reader and looks over three local newspapers every day, as well as reading *Time, Life* and *Reader's Digest* as soon as they hit the Reykjavik newsstands. In the last few weeks, he had also read *Old Man of the Sea, The Desperate Hours, Trial* and *The Man with No Name.* "Cowboy stories are favorites of mine, too," he said. "I get a chance to read them because so many of our books come from the States as paper-back books. And I like Mickey Spillane."

Icelanders have a saga literature dating back for centuries; the same stories, once told and retold in the long hours of the six-month winter night, are now printed and still popular in the same language in which they originated, exactly the same language that now appears on the pages of the daily newspapers. Isolation on this little island kept the language intact and made booklovers of the Icelanders. One teen-aged girl told me that she well remembered the long, dark winter days, without a glimmer of sunlight, when her aged grandmother in the north told the children story after story to while away the hours. In just the same manner, the first sagas were born. Now the people like old stories—and new— and there are twenty-three bookstores in Reykjavik alone.

Iceland also has several well-known authors, one a Nobel Prize winner and two whose books have been selected for the Book-of-the-Month Club.

Undoubtedly, some of the Icelandic love of books is due to the "long nights," the six-month period when the sun shows less and less each day until, in December, there is no daylight at all. Contrarily, June will find the sun shining brightly at midnight. "You just have to adjust," said Petur. "We were born to it, so we just keep on schedule. But strangers have to *make* themselves go to bed, even when the sky is bright."

Though he doesn't drink or smoke (American cigarettes here cost sixty-two cents a package), Petur has a sturdy appetite and after school often eats seconds of one of his mother's pet recipes, "doll's house pie." ("It's so easy to make," she explained with a laugh, "it's like playing doll house.") Butter, sugar and bread crumbs are molded into a lower crust, then spread with strawberry jam and sliced apples, baked and topped with whipped cream.

Out of the six ingredients of "doll's house pie," probably only the butter and whipped cream come from Iceland. The other items, including flour for the bread, plus thousands of other foodstuffs and manufacturing goods, are imported in the dark holds of the ships that come to port every day. Potatoes are grown on the island, as well as cabbage and some root vegetables; there are dairy and beef cattle and many sheep. Also, fish is plentiful, since Iceland probably has the best ocean fishing grounds in the world. But almost all other foodstuffs come from hundreds or thousands of miles away! Naturally prices are high: eggs cost about twelve cents each and such off-beat items as American-made fudge mix sell for $1.25 a box. However, nature—with tongue-in-cheek planning—has come up with a surprise to help out Icelandic menus: natural hot springs.

To counterbalance the thousands of acres of barren or ice-covered land where nothing will grow, other areas have natural underground hot springs that give Iceland an unexpected touch of luxury. This steaming water is simply piped in from the earth to towns and farmhouses for steam heating, hot water and even for heating green houses and chicken hatcheries. Glass hothouses often stand in the most barren fields, beaten by cold winds, with the inside as steamy as the tropics, filled with ripe tomatoes, tulips and even grapes. Tomatoes may be a Sundays-only delicacy and tulips cost fifty cents apiece, but they *can* be bought.

One chicken hatchery, built over hot springs right outside town, is run by a young Icelander who attended the University of Wisconsin. Outside, the wind tears fiercely at every fence and grass tuft; inside, the chicks are as warm and snug as under a mother hen's wing. Before World War II, many Icelandic students studied in universities in Denmark and Germany (the University at Reykjavik has 750 students, also); during and since the war, others went to school in the United States and have brought back business techniques and other skills.

Strangely, Iceland is a land almost completely without trees. The tallest scrub tree, carefully cultivated in towns, is about as high as a man's head and even grass patches are fenced and watched like tender flowers. All the wood for ship building or construction must be imported. Hence most buildings are made of cement blocks, then painted in enticing pastels—yellow, green, pink and a pale orange, to light up the bleak countryside. In centuries past, most buildings were made from thick squares of sod but now, except for an occasional rural cow shed, all such buildings have sunk back into the earth.

It is thought that Iceland had forest lands, far back in history, but wind, climate and time have brushed the earth flat. A treeless countryside, plus the eternal pushing winds, gives visitors the uneasy feeling of "falling off" the face of the earth and in the wide-open grasslands, where no obstacle mars the horizon, a traveler in a car has the sensation of hurtling into the beyond with the speedy, direct aim of a bowling ball.

Because there is no wood or other natural fuel source, the underground hot water supply saves the land: every house is snugly comfortable and water comes out of the "hot" faucets at near boiling point. It is strange, however, to see puffs of unchanneled steam crack through the barren earth in the countryside. At one point, where most of the ground was covered with snow, I stopped to wash my hands at a little hot water jet, just spouting up by itself through a snow-drift. And in another area, the marshy ground around a springlet was too hot to walk on.

This water supply also furnishes Iceland with its most popular sport: swimming. Most country schools have out-door warm-water pools and Reykjavik has two big public pools, indoor and out, open from seven in the morning till late at night. Many business men and students pop in for a swim before the day's work. One of the city pools has two sets of water jets, cold spouting in at one end, hot at the other. At a village school, miles inland, in the midst of a snow storm, I felt the water in a big, green-tiled outdoor pool. It was as warm and delightful as a Wisconsin lake on a hot July day.

Petur's favorite sports are skiing and skating, with an occasional salmon fishing trip with his father as a top treat. (Most of Iceland's best fishing streams are privately owned and rented out to sportsmen. A trio of Englishmen pays five thousand dollars per summer season for a choice spot.) With a school sports club, Petur and a group of boys take a nine-mile hike every second Saturday. Three times a year dances are held at school—"but nothing special," says Petur, "just dark suits for boys, and a little dancing."

Petur's junior year schedule doesn't leave much time for sports or dancing, however: with school five days a week, from eight o'clock till one-thirty, he crowds in a schedule of English, Icelandic, German, Danish, Latin, Chemistry, Mathematics, Geology, Gymnastics and Bookkeeping. "And next year—French," Petur explained. Since the Icelandic language is spoken nowhere else in the world, Icelanders are usually bi- or tri-lingual, speaking their own tongue, plus Danish and English. But Petur hopes to own a bookstore some day and he wants to be able to read and speak several languages.

"I've already clerked in bookstores during vacations," he said, "and I know a lot about running bookstores. One of the stores here was started by my grandfather and it is still in the family. That grandfather, incidentally, was Mayor of Reykjavik many years ago."

"Other summers, I've done other things," Petur went on. "Once I worked as a cook on a dredgeboat. I'm not a good cook, but I made a big Irish stew and that got me the job. I earned over $725 that summer!"

Jobs are easy to get in Iceland; in fact, many Icelanders say, "too easy for our own good." Right now, the island is plagued with the golden worry of over-employment: there are simply more jobs than people. Many workmen hold two or three separate jobs and there is not extensive leisure, even for the wealthiest people. (One prominent politician has a playboy son who spends his time loafing, drinking and driving around in a new car. He is criticized by the whole district, since the Icelanders are not usually lazy people.) Household help is extremely hard to get, with much of it imported from Denmark and Germany on generous terms: $25 a week, own room, regular free days, passage paid to Iceland, plus return passage, if the houseworker stays two years.

Unskilled labor, including occasional hookey teen-agers who skip school when a big boat comes in for unloading, earn upwards of seventy-five cents an hour, electricians and carpenters from $100 to $125 a week. There is so much work that many young marrieds can't get a night off unless their in-laws help out; nobody wants to baby-sit for only fifty cents an hour.

"I don't think it's good for us as a country," said Petur seriously, "to have things so easy. For instance, just a few weeks ago, a lot of cigarette butts were found in a shipment of frozen fish sent to a foreign market. In the old days, no one would be so careless. Now anyone knows if he gets fired, he can get another job tomorrow."

"And we have no army, navy or air force—so we have no compulsory military training. But I think *some* sort of compulsory training would be good for young people. Just a period of time in which one helped the country—youth training for working on the farms or building roads. We're getting careless and soft up here."

Petur is able to compare his country with others because he has made two extensive trips abroad. One year (with his "Irish stew money"), he visited Denmark and Sweden. The second trip, with an uncle-in-law who was once a Hungarian Communist, took him to England, France, Germany and Yugoslavia. "In Yugoslavia, we were allowed to do what we wanted, go where we wanted. The Communists were as nice to us as anyone else. But of course people are always curious to meet Icelanders. They are usually surprised that we're not Eskimos in furs!" (Many Icelanders are very tolerant to the idea of Communisim, the Communist party is a legal political party and in the last national elections, it polled twenty-two per cent of the vote. One reason for this tolerance is the fact that Russia is a big fish customer. Her trawlers fish off the shores and Icelanders see the country as a business associate, almost as a friend. However, after the recent anti-Communist riots in Hungary, Iceland quickly renewed her bid to the United States to stay on at the big Icelandic airbase.)

Most people of this island look and dress like prosperous Americans. Even in the country areas, the native costume is becoming rare, though occasionally older women may be seen in long, black skirts, white blouses with embroidered waistlets and tiny black tasseled skullcaps, like gay little cocktail hats. Most of the women and girls are astonishingly lovely, tall, slim and strong-looking, with fresh skin, clear eyes and shining hair. An average street crowd can produce two dozen girls who look like Hollywood starlets. On the other hand, the men seem warmhearted and intelligent—but few are as striking as the handsome girls.

Like most of his countrymen, Petur is a Lutheran. "Lutheranism is the state religion," says Petur, "but we are very liberal about this. We feel that we should go to church to be christened, confirmed and married." Even though legend says that Ireland's St. Patrick once landed on Iceland, there are only four hundred Catholics in the country now. Irishmen did, however, come to Iceland centuries ago, as slaves or captive brides, seized by marauding Danes and brought in by sea. The Icelanders still reflect an Irish sense of humor and—as shown by their laws—an interest in strong liquor.

"Without a doubt, one of the great problems in Iceland is our drinking," said Petur, self-critically. "It is not a problem with *me*—but many of my teen-aged boy friends like to drink until they lie on the floor. Why? I don't know. Because of the long winter nights? Because we are so alone on this island? I don't know."

But Icelanders *are,* on the whole, heavy drinkers. For a time the country experimented with a "Spanish prohibition," allowing only the sale of Spanish wines. (Spain is an important customer for Iceland's dried fish; Spanish wine was imported in return.) Now, however, liquor sale is state-controlled and only three places in Reykjavik have liquor licenses.

Besides being hard to get, liquor is very expensive. For instance, no alcoholic beer is allowed and American whiskey is twelve dollars a bottle, while a favorite local drink, *brennivin,* a potent, colorless liquid made from mash imported from Holland and fondly called "The Black Death," sells for $6.25 a bottle. *Brennivin* is often drunk plain, but some drinkers, including teen-agers, prefer it mixed with orange

[115]

juice, Coca Cola or coffee. Certain areas in Iceland have voted themselves "dry," such as the largest town in the north, Akureyri, with a population of 8,000. But, according to popular rumor, the cab drivers who meet the planes at the airport are also the local bootleggers and *brennivin* is not hard to come by, even though one may have to drink it while cabbing around town. "That's where the real trouble comes in, of course," explained Petur. "Liquor and cars."

Laws concerning liquor vs. driving are extremely strict, however; $500 fine for the first offense of driving "under the influence of liquor," whether an accident occurs or not, and loss of one's driver's license *for life* for a second offense. After a "coffee party" at the home of friends (drinks, coffee and six kinds of cake, drinks), many Icelanders prefer to take a taxi home and leave the family car till morning, rather than risk trouble with the local police.

Juvenile delinquency in the area is also chiefly associated with cars. Recently there was a spate of car looting by thirteen- and fourteen-year-olds and several boys of the same age group were caught borrowing cars for joy riding, while the owners were at the cinema. "That's why I say we need some sort of compulsory training," said Petur. "Young people are restless, they have too much money and not enough responsibility. This country is changing."

And why is little Iceland changing? The first big upsets began in World War II. At that time, Iceland was part of the political domain of Denmark. When the Germans under Adolf Hitler were overrunning Europe, Denmark was occupied. Then Britain—as protection for the non-Nazi world—moved her troops into Iceland. This isolated island suddenly became an important geographical point in the war. Later, many British troops were forced to withdraw to fight in Africa. At this point, Iceland, which has never had an army, invited the United States to send troops to the island. At one time there were 60,000 Allied troops in all encamped there. After peace was declared, Iceland joined NATO and allowed the United States to build a $100,000,-000 airbase at Keflavik, not many miles from Petur's home. Now 5,000 Americans and many planes, plus radar stations, barracks, giant PX's, bowling alleys and movie theaters are located at Keflavik. Naturally this all brings American dollars to Iceland—$13,000,000 every year paid out to Icelanders for labor, trucking services and dock facilities. (Though Icelanders and Americans are friendly, they rarely mix and the boys from Keflavik only leave the base on special pass. The reason is a simple one: Icelanders fear that 5,000 newcomers, changing every year or so, would have a restless, disrupting effect on the island. Hence most G.I.'s spend free time at the base, working hard and counting the days till they get back to the States.

During the war, hard-working Icelandic trawlers provided Great Britain with much of its fish food supply. As a fishing nation, with great trawler fleets, it has a prosperous fish trade and fisheries. Right now, the island's most important customers are Russia and the United States, with Russia leading as the bigger purchaser.

The air age has also changed the life of Iceland. In past years, Iceland could only be reached by lengthy boat trips through treacherous waters; now six major intercontinental flights land there each week, plus innumerable local flights, planes from Scotland, etc. (Iceland has always been a land of travelers and adventurers, however. In the year 1000, Leif

[117]

Erikson set sail for Greenland and eventually landed at the part of North America now called Nova Scotia.)

It is, therefore, the air age, the revenue from the Keflavik airbase and many prosperous years of fishing which have made Iceland a new-rich country. Richer and more restless. But for all the sudden changes in their lives, the tough, intelligent Icelanders are adjusting well.

"We have always been known as 'the independent people,'" said Petur. "We are known to be hard-working and hospitable. We are also a completely democratic nation, with no class distinctions. Anyone can be anything or marry anyone here. There is some distinction for the man who gets a better job—but that is a distinction he *earns.*"

Icelanders consider themselves a home-loving people and often say, "To understand our home life, you must see our kitchens." In the tiny village of Hvolsvelli, a cluster of eighteen houses set in the rough grazing country about thirty-five miles inland, a kind local citizen offered me coffee—and a tour of his kitchen—between buses. In his tiny, six-room house, overheated and spruced up for Sunday, we had two pots of coffee with five kinds of home-baked cakes, and then a look at the meticulous chrome and enamel kitchen. It had red inlaid linoleum and fluorescent lighting, plus a Danish stove and sink, a German cake-mixer and a Swiss sewing machine, lovingly covered with a fitted plastic hood. This small home—the head of the house is employed as a purchaser for a nearby cooperative store—also had six original oil paintings, several shelves of books and a large, highly colored wall tapestry of the Bay of Naples. And there were two radios.

Icelanders, in their wind-swept isolation, have a radio mania. Practically every home, and some of the local buses, has a radio, many with shortwave lengths which allow listeners to hear stations all over the world. The daily newspapers publish program schedules for eight neighboring countries. Thus Icelanders are among the hardest-listening, best-informed people in the world. Bridge and chess, natural entertainment for the long, dark months, are national favorites and the annual chess championship play-offs are broadcast by radio as avidly as our World Series. For a small fee, private funerals may also be broadcast and friends or relatives isolated by distance or the frequently bad roads can tune into services from home.

To see that well-equipped home in distant Hvolsvelli was like finding a soda fountain in the middle of the Sahara. I had taken a bus out of Reykjavik on a Saturday afternoon, planning to travel through the countryside for a few hours. It was late April, sunny but cold in town, with a wind so strong that it seemed to lay the land flatter, forcing people to lean toward buildings as they walked. Outside town, the fields were level, covered with a browned grass, cropped here and there by shaggy sheep or the squat, sturdy Iceland ponies. Later the landscape changed to mountains, many of black, curving lava that looked like the land of the moon. Soon we came to snow-covered fields. The narrow road here was rough and potted with muddy water-holes. Spray hit the windows till we couldn't see out, except for the tiny cleared opening round the driver's windshield wiper. Now and then, the snow in the fields was split by roaring gray streams, bubbling and churning—the wild, turbulent water from melted glaciers. Suddenly, the sunshine was dimmed by a flurry of snow, and wind rocked the bus. A few miles on, the driver stopped and several passengers struggled with snow chains, the whole group plastered white in a few seconds by the driving snow.

As we passed again into flat land, the snow swept across the road and our vision in straight sharp lines, like water falling down glass. Twice we went through villages, just clusters of houses sitting square and exposed in the wind. The rare farm house was only a glimmer of light, hidden in the snow. Just before we arrived at Hvolsvelli, the weather cleared abruptly and we drove into sunlight, a flat valley cupped in mountains, with a big snow-capped volcano, dominating the horizon. To emerge from the fierce blizzard was like winning a battle. There are no wild beasts in this country, but the weather that day seemed as wild and threatening to human life as a lion or a rampaging grizzly bear.

The day I left Iceland, Petur borrowed his father's green Oldsmobile to drive me on my way to the airport, talking and pointing out landmarks like an old friend. Later, looking down from the plane, little Iceland was like something made of rocks, blue paint and glistening white spun-sugar. Then came the curves of the shorelines, the dark, choppy gray of open sea. I felt like explorer Leif Erikson. I, too, had discovered a wonderful land.

7

MARIA MENDONCA

Portugal

"I KNOW I AM TOO FAT," said Maria Mendonca with a soft giggle, "but here we eat five times a day and I cannot leave alone those five o'clock teas with the big cakes!"

In many ways, Maria is a typical teen-ager, with her giggle, chubby figure, wardrobe of pretty pastel clothes and a mania for collecting Nat King Cole and Frankie Laine records. And in many ways she is a typical Portuguese, with a love of hard work, grave good manners and the deep, warm-hearted interest in religion that influences her whole life. Maria Mendonca is eighteen years old and lives in the bright, slick, sophisticated city of Lisbon, the capital of Portugal.

Portugal is a tiny country, only 100 miles wide, with the Atlantic on one side and the blue Mediterranean at the foot, and its entire length of 350 miles runs up the west side of Spain. However, the Portuguese are quick to say, "But we are very *different* from the Spaniards!" They like to think of themselves as more serious than their sunny, singing Spanish neighbors, a more energetic, determined people, with no time for afternoon siestas. This is a fresh, brilliantly sunlit land, where the lives of the people are never far from the ocean. It is a land of farmers and fishermen, working hard to haul the huge catches of sardines and tuna from the two seas and to cultivate the rocky, slanting fields along the mountain sides with olives, grape vines, fruit trees and cork oaks. Every portion of the land is put to use, and even the most barren, brown-green hillside is alive with the sound of shepherds' flutes and the jingling bells of the brown and white spotted goats.

As the United States is divided into forty-eight states, so the whole of Portugal is divided into twelve separate regions. However, in our country—except for a few minor differences—we all look, dress, talk and work in somewhat the same way. Not so in Portugal. In the big cities, fashions and customs are usually similar, but the peasant from the southernmost Algarve province and the fishermen from the seaside town of Nazare, in the province of Estremadura, nearly halfway up the Atlantic Coast, are distinctive types. The Algarve farmer rides to town in a gaily painted, four-wheeled cart, drawn by a horse with colorful balls and fringes on his harness and headgear. The farmer is stiffly and somberly dressed in narrow dark trousers, white shirt and dark beret or fedora; the women folk are severe-looking in their long black skirts, black blouses and black head scarves, over which are pulled down the same style black fedora hat that is sometimes worn by the men. Yet in Nazare, for example, the fishermen haul in the catch clad in bright or pastel wool plaid shirts and pants, the latter tightly pegged at the calf and bound at the waist with a colored wool sash. And their headgear is a cross between Old John Silver and Kris Kringle —a stocking cap of heavy wool cloth, usually a foot long and worn tight to the eyebrows. The women in this province choose black, too, but with full skirts underlined with many white petticoats, a black veil on the head and perhaps a brilliantly colored, wool-embroidered apron for holidays. In Portugal, interesting as the costumes of the various localities may be, the country people look "country" and the city people look "city," usually as tastefully dressed as the residents of such cities as Cleveland or San Francisco. But such dress differences tend to keep people apart by emphasizing class, work and locale separations.

Portugal is a dictator country, run since 1926 by an efficient and strong-willed ex-economics professor named Dr. Antonio de Oliviera Salazar. Though a new President of the Republic is elected every seven years, Dr. Salazar is the permanent Prime Minister. He is a dictator who lives quietly, rarely makes public appearances or allows his picture to be printed or hung and does not favor great shows of

military strength or uniformed, marching "youth move-
ments," as have many dictators in the past, but every
Portuguese knows that "no law, no appointment is valid
without his signature, his ideas become law." Yet in spite
of the natural diligence of the people and the determination
of the Salazar government to better the lot of the whole
population, this is still a poor country and only about five
per cent of the people have been able to attend school long
enough to read fluently, while forty per cent are completely
illiterate.

And this is where the bright young teen-agers like Maria
come in. "The sweet little ones—I so love children," she said
warmly and without affectation. "I have just finished the
first year of what you would call 'teacher's college.' I must
go to school one more year and then I will be a teacher for
the younger grades, what you would call a 'kindergarten
teacher.' I will teach in a school, probably here in Lisbon,
for one or two years and then—with friends of mine who
study with me now—I will try to open a nursery school of
my own. We have so few nursery schools, even in Lisbon."

The Instituto de Educaco Infantil, Maria's "teacher's
college," is a two-hundred-year-old house, once a wealthy
private home, set off a crumbling courtyard in one of the
oldest streets in Lisbon, not far from the town house of Dr.
Salazar. The heavy street door opens onto an enclosed garden
paved with worn cobblestones. Upstairs, the classrooms get
sunlight from ceiling-high windows and the walls are set
with ornate blue, white and orange mosaic tiles, reaching
several feet above the floor. But throughout the school, the
furniture and the equipment—plus the atmosphere and
teaching methods—are surprisingly modern. Two large

lecture rooms, equipped with blond wood chairs with desk-arms, are used for classes on child psychology, teaching techniques, play therapy and other subjects which will make good, modern-method teachers out of the thirty teen-aged girls studying at the school. The handicrafts rooms is a giant converted kitchen, with marble-topped tables and big sinks where the girls learn the tricks of crayons, clay and crêpe paper that amuse and train a young child. The reception room is decorated in bright print cotton, natural straw rugs and straw basket chairs with iron legs. Beside the chairs stands a big basket filled with colorful balls of yarn, knitting needles, knitted squares and a sign reading: "Other people are cold—why not knit while you wait?"

"This is a private school," Maria explained, "and each student must pay 200 escudos (about $6.50) a month to go here. We put out a school paper once a month," she said, indicating a mimeographed sheet of school news and gossip pinned on a bulletin board, "and once a week we have an all-school meeting, to make plans and iron out troubles. Each month we change school presidents, so everyone has a chance to act as a leader. We have fun here but we are really very serious."

The "seriousness" of the students is indicated by the tiny room used as a shrine dedicated to the Blessed Virgin Mary. (Though there is complete freedom of religion in Portugal, most people are Catholics and almost every Portuguese house has inset near the front door a big blue and white glazed tile, picturing the Blessed Virgin.) The little room is screened by a sliding curtain of blue cloth and fresh flowers and burning candles are kept before the simple statue of the

Virgin at all times. "Before exams," Maria laughed, "you have to wait in line for a turn to get in here to pray!"

In many ways, Maria's life as a student is strikingly similar to that of the average American high school student: she lives at home, is up at seven for a quick breakfast, at school all morning and home again at noon for a hasty lunch with the family. School in the afternoon, perhaps a short walk with girl friends before tea, then study in the bedroom until eight-thirty dinner, with an hour or two for study and radio music before bed.

"We have a house right in town," explained Maria, "and I share a bedroom with my sisters, Maria Leonor and Maria Helena, who are seventeen and fifteen. I could have a room all of my own—but who would want to miss all the fun?"

(The city of Lisbon is truly one of the most beautiful cities in the world. When approached by sea, it looks like a perfectly painted backdrop for a giant stage, with the houses and modern, balconied apartment buildings in white and pastel pink and green rising up the hills from the water's edge. But in Lisbon, like many big cities, there is a housing shortage and the government is building housing developments outside the city, to break up the population jam. The houses range from small four-room buildings to excellent six-room houses, with well-trimmed gardens. Public notice is put in the newspaper when each new building unit is begun and families must file application early to be considered. No one earning more than $107 a month is allowed in the developments and preference is given to large families, those living in extra-crowded conditions or otherwise in special need. Rent payments range from about seven to thirty dollars a month and the government absorbs the extra costs, allowing most families to own their house in a twenty-year payment period.)

"The first thing I do when I get home from school each day," says Maria, "is to turn on the radio. It is in the dining room but I turn it on so loud we can hear it all over the house. My parents get home later than I do—both are teachers in the public schools. You know, in most of Portugal, women do not work except with the children and in their own homes, but in the big cities, women sometimes like to work to help their husbands with things. When I marry, I hope I can keep working at my little school, too."

Mealtimes are always important in the Mendonca house because the Portuguese, who are usually rather small people, love to eat. "And with us," says Maria, "the mealtimes are for fun and talking. We even giggle at dinner." Tea time is at five o'clock and at that hour the chic sidewalk cafes of Lisbon are crowded with well-dressed women, having a cup of strong black coffee or tea with rich, fruit-filled pastries or cake; most men prefer a small glass of beer or white wine, with salted nuts or a few cold shrimp. The Mendoncas have tea at home and a larger evening meal, served around half-past eight. "We have a very good cook," says Maria, "and we usually have a thick vegetable soup, something with potatoes, onions, carrots and green peas, then a fish plate—a whitefish or a grilled sole with salad, then a meat plate, perhaps roast beef with fried potatoes and salad and cold meat. For dessert, either fruit or cheese—then coffee."

In Portugal, as in most countries where it is not always easy to make a living, food and eating are a very conspicuous part of life. Even the city dweller is conscious of the difficulty of raising food on slanting mountain sides, often tilled

[127]

with a horse and a handplow, or in fields kept green only through constant irrigation. The country roads, with lines of horsedrawn carts or peasants burdened with heavy baskets, and the outdoor markets where food must be brought fresh each day, keep the "food problem" constantly before the eye. Since most wages are low, people must work hard to earn enough to eat—and thus like to eat well when they can. For instance, in Lisbon one day, in a small simple restaurant on a side street, crowded with oilcloth-covered tables, we saw a big workman eat slowly, and with great relish, for a full hour. He began with enough *caldeirada mista* to fill two deep soupbowls. This is a fish stew, made from white fish, squid, shrimp, eels, potatoes, onions and sweet peppers, all in a thick brown gravy. Then came a platter of fried steak, decorated with slices of lemon and wheels of butter, French fried potatoes and green beans, followed by a salad of sliced tomatoes, raw onions and cucumbers, with oil and vinegar, and a third of a loaf of bread. Dessert was a platter of fruit—grapes, figs and melon slices—and a thick wedge of goat cheese. During the meal, the man emptied a quart bottle of red wine and he cleaned each plate completely, except for the occasional scrap he tossed to the restaurant cat! Judging from his muscles and roughened hands, he had worked hard to earn the meal and the right to enjoy it.

Despite many similarities, there is one way in which Maria's life is completely unlike that of most American teen-agers: she has no household chores and does no housework of any kind. Even in her moderate income home, there is a cook and a maid-of-all-work who do everything from cooking and shopping to the house-cleaning and sewing on of buttons. "They are girls from the country who want to live in the city," explains Maria. And though Maria is not likely to say so, they are also girls willing to work hard simply for a place to sleep and enough to eat—on wages of between five and ten dollars a month. For girls with suffi- cient education or special training, there is usually work to be found, but in Portugal children are required by law to go to school only to complete the primary grades—that is, until they are about ten years old. The Salazar government has dotted the countryside with new primary schools and almost every small town has a neat white school house, usually set in a gravel play yard, with a trim of red geraniums. But education beyond the primary grades becomes expensive.

As a family, the Mendonca girls are distinguished by their strong drive for a good education. Though the youngest girl has not made up her mind about a career, Maria Leonor is in her first year of study as an electrical engineer and Maria herself, under her ultra-feminine exterior of dimples, perfect manicures and pale pink dresses, which she loves, has some firm ideas about "doing good in life." Much of her interest in modern education comes from the director of the Instituto de Educacao Infantil, Maria Teresa Andrade Santos, who studied child education in Portugal, England, Switzerland and the United States. Though Miss Santos herself is pretty and gay, she also gives her students a clear idea of the hard work that lies ahead in bringing even simple education to more Portuguese. She herself sets an interesting example.

"In the school months, of course, I am busy with classes," explained the teacher, "but in the summer months several 'older' young women like myself—a couple of teachers, a couple of doctors—set out by car for one of the very remote mountain villages, to see what we can do for the people.

[129]

Many of these people, out of touch not only with the progress of Portugal but of the whole world, have nothing in their lives—no electricity, no machinery—just life in a primitive village, usually without a school or church of any kind. Our group rents a simple house in the village, tries to teach the children a little, talks to the villagers about religion (many have not seen a priest in years) and finds out what can be done to help them—perhaps through medicine, perhaps by trying to get the government in Lisbon to help with an irrigation system or some farming plan. We cannot do much in a short time but these people are so grateful for any help that our house is like a clubhouse. The women, even the poorest, bring us little gifts of food and one night the men took the only lantern from the town tavern down the village street to our house to join the hymn singing. After the singing, they all went back to the tavern but they *did* come! The suicide rate is very high in these remote villages because the people often despair, so out of touch with help and change—just living on the end of a narrow dust road that wandered off the main road. But little by little, with many people helping, we may be able to do some good." It is this strong feeling of responsibility that shows itself in the classrooms at the Instituto de Educacao Infantil and makes Maria Mendonca's face become serious when she talks about her future plans for work with "the little ones" and "my school."

But, of course, Maria also has fun in her life. Her family owns a small house by the seashore, not far from Lisbon, where they vacation every summer for the months of July and August. (Just outside Lisbon, too, is the famous seaside resort area of Estoril, one of the wealthiest, most glamorous spots in the world. Mile after mile of graceful villas stretch along the curve of white-sand Atlantic beaches, with night clubs, restaurants and a gambling casino twinkling lights and echoing dance bands into the early morning. Many "retired" kings and queens of Europe now make their homes in Estoril and it is a favorite vacation spot for play-folk from all over the world.)

"At the seashore," says Maria, " I do nothing but play and rest for my studies for the next year. I love to swim and we sometimes play badminton. Then I have my hobbies—I collect stamps, postcards and match covers. And, of course, I read. My father likes the news, so I sometimes look over three or four papers a day, though I don't always read the serious things. (The newspapers in Portugal are strictly censored under the Salazar government, but the censorship affects chiefly news about Portugal, its colonies and its internal affairs, all of which are reported thoroughly and always in favorable terms. An American government official living in Lisbon remarked, "I get bored so quickly with the Portuguese newspapers because they print so little *real* news and so little news about the rest of the world. I think you can always tell a dictator country by the amount of sports and movie articles used to stuff the newspapers.")

Maria studied English for four years in school and speaks it easily, just as she does French. English and American pocket-size books are popular and cheap in Lisbon and she likes to read historical romances and such round-the-world mystery favorites as Ellery Queen, Erle Stanley Gardner and Agatha Christie.

The Avenida de Liberdade, a long, elegant boulevard that cuts through the center of Lisbon, shady with palm trees and sweet with flowers, is a favorite spot with the young

Lisbonese, for promenading and group dates. The center boulevard strip is lined with bright tables and chairs for refreshments or for that variation of a favorite European pastime, "watching the crowd go by." In such places as Rome, Madrid and Paris (as well as smaller towns), young people love to dress in their best clothes, go promenading up and down the main streets on a sunny afternoon or just sit in a sidewalk cafe with a lemonade, watching the other promenaders. In Lisbon, where wealthy men often like to show the extent of their bank accounts by the number and size of their cars, the cafe sitters are treated to a parade of shiny, expensive automobiles whizzing by, everything from sleek red Jaguars to solemn, glossy American Cadillacs.

At one end of the Avenida is the "Greenhouse," a sprawling, roofed garden—formerly an old stone quarry—full of brooks, birds, exotic plants, trees and flowers, and little paths and benches which make it an ideal date spot for groups of teen-agers. And along the Avenida are several of the plushiest movie theaters in town. Movies are big-time entertainment in Lisbon and on week-ends or holiday nights, many adults go to the late movie in complete evening dress, stopping at a cafe or night club afterward. Most movie theaters are equipped with little coffee bars for a pick-up during the "intermission" in the movie. Portugal is very class-conscious and the women usually choose elaborate clothes, jewelry and heavy make-up for evening wear, leaving the simple cottons and sandals for the girls in the country.

"I am allowed to go to the movies once a week," explained Maria. "Sometimes even more. Most of the movies are in English, you know, with Portuguese subtitles, so I am also learning something when I go. (In most parts of Europe,

American and English movies are shown with a native language soundtrack, rather than in the original English.) My favorite movie stars are Esther Williams and Frank Sinatra. I think the favorite movie star of all Portugal is Gregory Peck!"

But like any carefully brought up Portuguese girl, Maria is never allowed to go out on dates alone and will not be until she is engaged to be married. "We do it this way," she explained. "Sometimes we all go—a group of boys and girls together—to an afternoon movie. Usually each one pays for himself but sometimes a boy pays for a girl, if she is his favorite. We sometimes have little parties at someone's home for dancing, but usually in the afternoon. I love all kinds of dancing but have never taken lessons. We never go out in the evening except with our parents. What we call 'the afternoon' really ends at eight o'clock, but with my parents I have been out till one!"

The Portuguese teen-agers seem as concerned as their parents about keeping these severe dating rules and there is little chance of slipping off to cafes or parks for secret dates. A boy would probably think less of a girl, in this strict society, for doing it. As a small example of the standards of the country, take the matter of bathing suits on public beaches: no two-piece suits are allowed for women and no man or boy over ten years of age is allowed on a public beach in swimming trunks alone. Should a male tourist fail to observe this regulation, a beach guard firmly suggests that he rent a white jersey swimsuit top at once—or go back to his hotel.

"We live more 'at home' than girls in the United States," Maria said. "We study harder but we stay children longer.

For instance, few of us in the group would ever have a part-time job or make any money ourselves until we are out of school. I don't have an allowance. I just ask my father when I need something but he is very generous and I get more that way. Portuguese girls do not do baby-sitting for money (it is so easy to have a little maid) but sometimes we do tutoring for younger students and get paid for that. Our parents support us and rule us, even though they are very kind, until we get married."

Even though she has never had a date in the usual teen-aged sense, Maria is confident and eager to get married—"but not until I am twenty-two or twenty-three. I would like to marry a doctor or an engineer. The face does not matter so much but I would like him to love music, the cinema, reading and sports. And I would like him to be kind, nice and clever."

In Portugal, where opportunity is still limited, most people manage to be happy with what they can get. Maria has no bright lights dreams for herself, no fierce drive for fame, no need to wander around the world. She has clearly decided what work she wants to do and she wants to do it in her own country.

"I think," Maria said seriously, "that girls all the world over are alike, with some small things changed for each country and race. I am Portuguese but I like all people. I hope my answers about my life will help Americans to understand and love Portuguese girls."

8

PEPE GOMEZ

Canary Islands

YOUNG, DARK-EYED Pepe Gomez of the Canary Islands has
never heard of Christopher Columbus. Yet almost five
hundred years ago that famous explorer stopped at these
rugged, flower-scented islands to hear Mass and to fill the
water casks of his ships before setting sail on the long voyage
to America. Pepe has neither time nor money for history.

He is seventeen years old, has never gone to school a day in his life and on the forty-seven cents a day he earns as a banana plantation laborer, he could never afford to buy a history book.

Yet life seems good to Pepe these days. Things are certainly better now with the Gomez family than when he was a little boy. All the Gomezes were born here, near Las Palmas on Gran Canaria, the largest of these Spanish-owned islands. It is a rough, mountainous butt of land, jutting out of the sea only seventy-two miles from the northwest coast of Africa. These Canary Islands—seven in all—are so small that on the map of the world they look like no more than a few dots and dashes in the Atlantic Ocean. But in reality, they are a busy, crowded crossroads for ships of all nations.

For most of his life, Pepe and his family lived in a one-room cave home, part of the sprawling, squalid cave village on the rocky slopes above the port city of Las Palmas. The cave was a natural hole in the rock, raw and damp, without light, heat, plumbing or water. Señor Gomez built a shack-like porch of dried sugar cane around the cave door and his wife planted shoots from wild geraniums about the stony bit of front yard so the flowers blazed red twelve months of the year. But it was still a makeshift, impoverished home, dreary and chill.

Fortunately, Pepe can remember some good things about life in that cave: days of playing with other children on the mountainside when the weather was mild and warm and the great view of the Atlantic with black freight steamers and sleek white tourist boats sailing in and out of the harbor night and day. The islands and the mountains have a brilliant, picture-postcard beauty, but Pepe can remember misery, too—more misery than beauty. He will never forget the fiercely cold dampness of the winter months, the thinness of his cotton clothes, the fog swirling and dipping over the mountains, with only the small cooking fire in the cave for warmth. He will never forget the hours of scouring the mountainside for bits of twig and heavy fern to feed the fire and the long struggle up the rocks twice a day with heavy earthenware jugs of drinking water from the stream below. And he remembers clearly how often he and his brothers were hungry.

In those days, Senor Gomez walked four miles each day, to and from work on a banana plantation, earning about $3.60 a week. Senora Gomez labored during every daylit hour on intricate hand embroidery. A large tablecloth with twelve matching napkins sometimes brought nine dollars from a tourist shop near the Las Palmas docks. Still there was never quite enough money to buy bread, mutton, onions or fish, to keep the family fed. Pepe never got used to the ache of hunger though. He has the wiry energy of a mountain boy but his body, at seventeen, though muscular, is slight, thin and somewhat stunted.

Yet the sun does shine in the Canaries, not only on the flowering mountain peaks and the tourist beaches, but into the dark lives in the caves. Two years ago, life changed for the Gomezes. First, they moved into a new home and second, Pepe was lucky enough to get work with his father in the banana fields. Their new home is in a government-financed housing development, built on the low, warmer mountain slopes just above the city. (The flat land nearer the sea is saved for planting banana trees, since the fruit grows and matures in only seven months in these ideal fields.) The

[137]

housing development is made up of several streets of apartment buildings and row after row of tiny single houses, all
constructed of stone and stucco painted in fragile shades of
blue, pink or green. There is electricity and running water
and a wood-burning stove for cooking. Senora Gomez has
again planted the front yard with geraniums and a double
row of sunflowers that stretch as high as the little house.
(Nothing is wasted here. The sunflower seeds are roasted,
salted and used for food.) The family of five is jammed into
two small rooms, but the Gomezes feel lucky and very proud.
Not all the mountain cave families have been able to crowd
into the new settlement and the monthly rental for the little
pink house comes to about seventy-five cents. Now Pepe and
his parents are saving for the day when they can buy beds.

Pepe got his job at the banana plantation because his
father had been a good worker and because, after an especially good year, the plantation took on new hands. Sometimes his working days stretch from eight o'colck in the
morning until long after dark and his weekly wages come to
less than three dollars, but Pepe is glad to have the work.
He knows how many men are without employment, not only
teen-agers but older men, hanging around the docks, hoping
to earn a few pesetas loading wagons or carrying baggage.
Even though the Canary Islands are prosperous as ports,
sending huge shipments of fresh fruits and vegetables all
over the world, there are still more willing men than there
are jobs.

Pepe likes his work. The short, straggly banana trees reach
just over his head and the coarse, feathery leaves make a
complete canopy as he moves between the trees. At all times,
the ground must be kept loose and carefully hoed. Ordinary

[138]

kitchen garbage, chopped fine, is mixed with the earth around the roots as fertilizer, and a narrow groove is kept open between the neat rows of trees, to be used whenever irrigation is necessary. The ditches are necessary, too, when the heavy rains of the winter months pound and swamp the earth.

Pepe has learned how to prune and care for the sensitive trees, to keep them producing; each tree will bear one blossom and one bunch of bananas in its lifetime, so to maintain a profitable, working plantation, "three trees" must be kept growing out of each root at all times. There is the "grandfather tree," on which the bunch of green bananas is growing, the "father tree," which is nearly full-sized and almost ready to blossom, and the "son tree," a little sprout which will have about eight months to grow before it becomes the "father tree" and that tree steps up one degree in the family. Bananas are always shipped green and it is part of Pepe's job to cut through the heavy black stalk and load the bananas on donkey-drawn carts, to be carried to the plantation sheds for packing. As soon as a bunch of bananas is cut, that tree is also cut down and a new shoot forced up from the root so the "three tree" cycle is never broken. At this plantation, some of the roots have been producing trees and bananas for over sixty years.

Sometimes Pepe rides into Las Palmas in the cab of the truck used to deliver crated bananas to the docks for loading on the cargo boats. Along the docks, the huge cranes bend and creak like giant insects, lifting boxes and bales with tireless rhythm, loading the holds of ships for the long journey to the markets of the world. On these rare visits to town, Pepe gets a glimpse of other worlds, worlds very

[139]

different from the little two-roomed pink house or the isolated, shady rows of banana trees. From the ships along the docks come wealthy Spaniards, handsomely dressed, well-educated men visiting the islands for a vacation or on business, English tourists who are probably the most common foreign visitors to the sunny Canaries and even a few Americans. (The Americans usually seem as wealthy as kings to Pepe—not only because they can afford to travel so far from home but because some of them even bring their cars.)

Pepe is often self-conscious and shy in this big port town and among strangers. He lived too long in the mountain caves and he is conscious of the fact that he cannot read and can barely write his own name. But like most Spaniards, he is always courteous and well-mannered. He has been taught at home to say *buenos dias* when greeted and he can say it with grace and charm, even to staring tourists who want to snap his picture. And he is handsome in his faded blue shirt and rolled-up trousers, his bare feet in black cloth sandals with cactus-fiber soles and a small black beret tipped on the back of his head. But he does not look like a city boy. Even standing among the trucks and humming cranes, there is a wiry wildness about him. He has never quite lost the lonely look of the mountain people. (On one high part of the island, there lies the crater of an extinct volcano, a deep, broad scoop in the earth, miles wide, covered over now with grass and a few neat farming fields. At the bottom, like children's toys, sit two small farmhouses and a cluster of outbuildings. Here lives an old farmer and his son with his young wife. So remote is the life, that all food is raised in this isolated crater and the families usually make only two trips a year up the rugged slopes into town. The trail to the top, and the outside world, is no more than a shadow brushed through the grass and shrubs.)

However, in the city of Las Palmas there are many comfortable residential streets, shaded with palms; big white stucco, balconied houses are set back in gardens magnificent with flowers and blossoming vines and shrubs. On the business streets, there are good shops, cinemas and sidewalk cafes and the cluster of souvenir shops selling ivory elephants, cheap perfumes and bright silk pajamas from Japan. But these spots represent unattainable luxuries to Pepe. There is little excitement in his life except the bright scenery and the pleasure of sea and sun when the weather is good. His working day is too long and his wages are too low for much else.

What does he do for fun? Occasionally he goes to a cockfight but he has never gone to a movie, has never been on a boat and has never gone to a "party," except perhaps to join the neighborhood crowd and watch religious processions in the village squares on church holidays. On such fiesta days, Pepe and his two brothers prefer to go to church in one of the mountain villages, rather than in bustling Las Palmas. Sometimes they go with their mother to the famous church of the Virgin of the Pines, high in the hills, built on a site where the Blessed Virgin Mary is believed to have appeared to some Spanish soldiers over five hundred years ago. In the comparative poverty of the village, the church stands out with dazzling splendor, old but graceful and full of treasures. Above the altar rests a statue of the Blessed Virgin, dressed in gold-embroidered cloth, a crown of diamonds and rubies on her head and all ten fingers of her plaster hands sparkling with rings. Pepe (like most people of the area) has great faith in the Virgin of the Pines and he credits his mother's prayers to the Virgin for intercession with her Son with getting him his job.

It takes three special rooms behind the altar (plus some space in local bank vaults) to hold the gifts to the Virgin from other pious Spaniards who feel she has answered their special prayers. Glass cases, carefully locked, glitter with gifts, such as altar vessels in pure gold, decorated with precious stones from the personal jewel case of some grateful Señora. There are intimate gifts like wedding rings, emerald earrings, bracelets, tiny jeweled crosses and even a set of sapphire cuff links, still in their satin-lined box, marked with the name of a Madrid jeweler. In a special showcase there is a dramatic collection of bullets removed from the bodies of wounded soldiers who prayed and lived—and then made a pilgrimage to the church of the Virgin of the Pines to give their gifts and thanks.

In a tiny room, just beyond the display of precious gifts, is a poignant display of the faith that fills these island people. It is a collection of wax shapes, hung by ribbons from a kind of huge bulletin board: a waxen ox, a gnarled hand, a baby's body, a slim girl's leg and many other shapes. As is customary on the islands (and in many parts of Spain), a devoted churchgoer may put his request to the Virgin into wax (prayers for an ailing baby, a sick cow, an arthritic hand, etc.) and hang it near the splendid statue of the Virgin, hoping that his plea will be remembered and answered. At the Virgin of the Pines church, most of the "wax prayers" are molded for a small fee by the sexton, who also happens to be a fairly good sculptor, able to shape a rheumatic leg as realistically as a shapely one. The wax shapes hang mutely, discolored by age and the smoke of incense from the altar, touching reminders of the tragedies that have touched village life. Only faith and little wax images through the decades—and no sign as to the way in which the prayers were answered.

On religious fiestas, Pepe and his brothers hear Mass first, then spend the rest of the day lounging around the village square, sometimes chipping in a few pesetas (there are about thirty-eight pesetas to a dollar) to buy a package of cigarettes or a bottle of good Spanish beer, each costing about ten cents. With the better family income, holidays now mean a special dinner at home, too—perhaps garlic and tomato soup with a raw egg in each bowl, a bit of mutton cooked with carrots, onions and round mealy peas and bananas or a few cactus pears Señora Gomez has gathered on the mountainside. The luxury of a full meal is still rare for Pepe, but his forty-seven cents a day has definitely changed life for the Gomez family. His younger brothers are not as hungry as he was. Perhaps the youngest will even go to school—if there is enough money for shoes and a warm jacket. And if a school can be built in time.

At the moment, young Pepe's worries are small because his luck seems big. To a seventeen-year-old who has never seen beyond the fifty-by-thirty mile boundaries of his island home, a full meal plus the warm Atlantic sun can make the future look very bright.

9

JODY REGAR

Nouasseur Air Base, Morocco

TODAY THERE ARE new silhouettes on the bright blue horizons around the old town of Casablanca. As relics of the earlier days, tall, slim minarets are still etched against the sky, along with the newer, chalk-white apartment buildings and sleek hotels built by the French that stand, as modern and glistening as rows of ice-cube trays, while in the dusty stretch of fields outside town, the great beige camels plod and sway under their burdens as they have for centuries past.

But now, south of Casablanca, from the United States Air Base at Nouasseur, jets and fighter planes flash like bright silver crosses through the sky—a new sight and sound over colorful Morocco. Nouasseur, part of a gigantic defense building project in which $500,000,000 has been spent in Morocco alone, is one of the five airbases constructed by the United States in this far-off country of camels and casbahs.

Jody Regar lives at Nouasseur. "At least I live here *now,*" she explained with a laugh, "and I've been here for over nine months—but I'm an army brat and I just live wherever Daddy is assigned."

Lieutenant Colonel P. W. Regar is an army engineer attached to the Nouasseur Base, one of 15,000 American military personnel and their dependents now living in Morocco. Jody is an only child, a tall, graceful seventeen-year-old, who could cover her suitcases with travel stickers and fill a dozen diaries with notes about her army travels. Jody is a new kind of teen-ager and a new kind of American, one of the thousands of United States citizens who have penetrated other lands through our military friendships, bringing examples of the American way of life—plus airfields, fighter planes and new political responsibility—to areas from wind-swept Iceland to sun-parched Libya.

"You get used to traveling and you get used to making new friends," Jody explained philosophically. "I was born in Waynesboro, Pennsylvania, but we've always shifted around. For three years—between the time I was ten till I turned fourteen—we lived in Japan. First Tokyo, then Yokahama. Many of my friends were American army children, but I got to know and love the Japanese (what wonderful buildings they have in that country—so clean and cool!) and my music teacher was a White Russian!"

"After Japan, we were reassigned to the United States and I had a couple of years to make friends down in Wilmington, North Carolina. At first, here at Nouasseur, everyone was new to me—but now I feel completely at home. Because of all the political trouble, it's hard to make friends with the natives here, but the other day I met a Jewish-Moroccan girl through my music teacher and she invited me to her home in the casbah. Little by little, wherever we've moved, we've met someone new. I'm lucky to love music because in each country there are people who love music, too. Schubert and Brahms are almost a universal language."

It was a brilliantly hot August day but Jody sat cool and fresh in a linen dress as blue as the cloudless sky. Outside, the airbase was spread flat and wide in the sun. Located on Moroccan soil, built with the permission of the then-governing French, constructed by American plan and taxes, this base does not even fly the American flag. But it stands as a link in a defensive chain to protect the free world. The residential area is like an animated toy village, with orderly, right-angle streets, few buildings over one story tall, shiny American cars flashing, and housewives burdened with supermarket groceries rushing from the curbside into the little houses. Here and there, off-duty soldiers, casual and well-groomed, stroll toward the baseball field, the post office or the PX.

Jody has just finished an eight-to-five working day as a typist and file clerk with the Atlas Construction Company, the contractors whose bulldozers and steamrollers are laying out the five airbases on the flat Moroccan plains. Just two months before, Jody was graduated from the airbase high school, one of a class of eighteen seniors. The yearbook pointed her out as "The Prettiest Girl" and "The Most Popular," but it didn't add that she is probably also the hardest working teen-aged girl on the base.

"About the only thing I didn't like about the high school here was the fact that we didn't have to work enough. Senior year was more like ninth grade to me. We had eighty-eight students in the whole high school—boys and girls from everywhere, everyone trying to catch up or keep up.

"But graduation was perfect, just like any graduation in the States—all pomp and sentiment. We held it at the base chapel and afterward Mother and some of the other mothers gave a buffet supper at the TCV (Temporary Construction Village club). We had the whole class, plus one guest each. I asked my English teacher as my guest. He has a wonderful sense of humor and we all wanted him there. And there are ten boys in the senior class to seven girls—so all the gals always feel sort of special."

Life for teen-agers at Nouasseur is a mixture of luxury and boredom, a combination of camping out and living in a small but wealthy town. Unmarried soldiers are quartered in crowded barracks on one part of the base, while married personnel and married construction workers live with their families in another area, in diminutive, one-story houses that look makeshift and temporary on the outside, but are comfortable and colorful within. The streets are smoothly paved, like any suburban streets, but the sidewalks leading to the houses are usually flat planks, cutting through a bit of green lawn and bordered with such sprawling flowers as geraniums or nasturtiums.

Colonel Regar's house is of gray clapboard, five-roomed, one-storied and small. Like most of the houses on the base, it looks very "American" on the inside, with a gleaming kitchen, good bathroom and mechanical household aids. Jody's mother has chosen to decorate mostly in antiques (most army personnel ship their household goods from post to post), a few Japanese ornaments, low coffee tables and chests of drawers and some ivory-colored goatskin ottomans bought in Casablanca.

"Mother and Daddy gave me the biggest of the bedrooms," said Jody, "because I like to spend so much time in it, just sitting around with the girls after school." Besides the bed, there is a comfortable chaise longue and the room is decorated in white, with red and white, tiny-checked taffeta and white ruffles.

"For all the the teen-agers here, the main problem is finding something to do," explained Jody, "and for some of us that problem is serious."

Seven years ago, the site of Nouasseur was nothing more than flat fields and one small, impoverished Arab village. Now it is a complicated, highly mechanized, very busy airfield, with barracks, workshops, hangars, houses, stores and acres of jeeps, trucks, planes and other machines. Yet teen-agers (or other non-qualified personnel) are not allowed on many parts of the base, so they beat well-worn paths between school, home, the PX, the Teen Club and the movies. It is like living in a small town where one is only allowed to walk along the Main Street. And Casablanca itself lies a good half hour's drive away. It is a glamorous town, almost cut in half by current political troubles. The medina or fascinating walled native living quarters are completely off bounds for military personnel and, at critical times, the whole town plus the nearby beaches are considered dangerous and restricted. (Most Arab rage is directed toward the French, but riots, knifings and bombings render the whole area tense. And some months ago an Army captain, returning to Nouasseur from Casablanca by car at night, was stopped on the highway and shot dead without explanation.)

"Most of us—well, we're just a bunch of kids living with our parents, but we don't really live here in the sense that we *belong*," explained Jody. "At school, for instance, we have no real sports or clubs, and just a mimeographed newspaper. Nothing you can get all wrapped up in. When we get home at night, there is just nothing to do but have a soft drink, listen to records—and talk. Lots of the teen-agers' mothers have office jobs here on the base, so they aren't here when the kids get home. Even girls fall into the habit of one or two cans of beer after school out of boredom.

"Most of us don't even have any housework we can do. The houses are small and almost everyone has a Fatima, anyway." ("Fatima" is the local nickname for housemaids—and also a highly revered name among Moslems, since Fatima was the daughter of the great Moslem prophet, Mohammed. Most of the maids live in the casbah area of Casablanca, commuting to and from the base each day, shuffling about the little houses, hard at work in traditional flowing white garments and pastel leather backless slippers. In the house, these women may go unveiled, but while huddled around the bus-stops and on the streets of Nouasseur, they are discreet, withdrawn and veiled to the eyes. The average salary for a Fatima is two dollars a day, a good wage in this low-wage country.)

"I make my own bed in the morning," said Jody, "just to give myself something to do. Half the time we don't even cook at home. There are only the three of us and we can have dinner in the evening in the mess hall. For mother and me, the charge is just forty cents each and the menu always has roast beef, steak or chicken, plus vegetables and other things. Occasionally I bake at home on the week-ends, to have something to do. Cakes or cookies. But I never touch them myself!"

"Daddy cooks sometimes, too—charcoal steak with sauce or even Baked Alaska. But he doesn't eat much, either, because an officer can't be fat."

(Food shopping at a U.S. army base PX is like pushing a cart through a supermarket planned by Hollywood: the most popular American foods, from frozen pizzas to instant mixes, are stacked four deep on the shelves; American-type bread is baked especially for the base and such essentials as shampoos, cigarettes, Kleenex, liquor and chewing gum are stocked by the dozens. Naturally, since one PX will supply the whole base, it is organized so that the stock won't run short. To a native of a country where workers may earn as little as fifty cents a day, the PX makes all Americans look like kings.)

On the base, a big quonset hut has been converted into The Teen Club and all eighty-eight high school students have become members, with dues of fifty cents a year. "We have movies, bingo, dances, badminton, French lessons, use of the pool—everything we need except enough real work to fill our time," complained Jody. "And we're just the same old people all the while."

"Naturally, everyone is glad to get a job in the summertime and luckily there is work for everyone right here on the base, from helping with surveying to secretarial work. And what salaries! Girls usually earn from $250 to $300 a month, and it's $300 and up for boys. Some fellows I know have earned up to $600 a month with overtime!"

Much of the labor on the base is done by Arab workers, with only the higher, specialized help imported from the United States. These native workers earn much less than the Americans (the wage scale was set by the French under the original agreements for building the bases) and they do not live on the base, but return to town each night by truck or bus. Thus, besides a language barrier, many Arabs and Americans are kept apart because they cannot become friends after hours or on the same income level.

"I've seen as much of the country as I can—under the conditions," Jody explained. "We've driven to Marrakesh (the beautiful inland city, ringed with mountains and famous for its squares, fountains and buildings of pale red clay). I visited the market place, the gold market and had some of the wonderful native food—chicken, pigeon pie and mint tea.

"But almost everywhere I go the atmosphere is French. All the good hotels and restaurants are French. Most of the people we meet off the base are French. Most of the movies, theaters, newspapers—everything of that type—is in French. We live in Morocco, but the culture we see most is French."

(Morocco, after being under harsh French protectorate for decades, gained its independence only in March, 1956. Many Frenchmen still run the businesses of Morocco and French soldiers police the country, still immensely stronger than the new Moroccan army. Negotiations for building the

[151]

U.S. airbases here were made between Washington and Paris and the Sultan of Morocco was not even consulted. Even though the Americans and Moroccans are now in close and friendly contact, there is still bitter feeling against all "foreigners" in the country. Travelers are warned not to travel at night, to keep out of the medinahs and off back country roads—and to avoid crowds.)

Luckily for Jody, she need not spend one empty sunny hour in Morocco. She can keep herself busy getting ready for the future. Three hours a day minimum is the music practice time she sets for herself, for she hopes someday to see the name "Jody Regar" on a program as a concert violinist.

"I have always loved music," she explained. "When I was a little girl—only about six—I remember lying on an old studio couch, listening to my father play, and I thought he was the most wonderful man in the world.

"With all our moving around, I've already studied under ten different teachers. Each Saturday afternoon, right now, I go into Casablanca for lessons in technique and in theory of music. In the fall, I will go each day to the Casablanca Conservatory. I know I will find that wonderful. I'll be studying with Arab and French students, so I'll really get to know something of the customs and languages.

"In Japan, for instance, I was part of a chamber group, and those musical associates became my most important friends."

Among Jody's crowd of much-traveled teens, names of cities such as London, Munich and Madrid are dropped just as casually as Chicago, Illinois, or Fall River, Nebraska, are among U.S. teens. "A group of us in the graduating class decided to meet in Paris for a reunion in one year—just to see what's happened to us all! After that, I hope to study at Julliard in New York—till I'm ready for Carnegie Hall," she added with a laugh.

Jody is a determined, thoughtful and orderly worker and, though her talent as a violinist may or may not allow her to bow to Carnegie applause, she works at life now as if she were already a concert star. This is the fourth summer that she has held a full-time job, yet never once missing out on three hours of violin practice a day. Her school grades were at the top of the class and she is an inveterate reader, though she sees only occasional movies. "I find I can cry just as easily over a good book!"

In appearance, she is a phenomenon of good grooming: a pretty girl whose excellent care makes her seem even prettier than she is.

"Mother has always been nice-looking," Jody explained, "and she is a superb housekeeper. She calls herself just a good Dutch housewife but I think she should be managing a huge plantation! And being an army officer, Daddy's a fanatic about neatness. So I just grew up in the habit of being tidy!"

At five feet-seven, Jody is a slim, long waisted 118 pounds who can eat anything she wants "except what's bad for my skin." (In the last few months, Jody has been suffering from a slight case of acne. She takes this blemish very seriously and is following the advice and diet prescribed by a base doctor.)

"I'm just a soap and water girl," she said. "But I like a lot of that. And I set my own hair every other night." Jody's light blonde hair is worn smooth, pulled away from the face and held in soft, simple curls on her neck.

"It's on clothes that I go haywire," she said "and I must have spent $500 on this summer's clothes alone. Mother and Daddy give me a $10 a month allowance and the rest of the money I earn myself. I'm a size ten, even in length, and I often pay a lot for clothes I like and then take good care of them. My winter coat cost $125 and I have one formal that cost $150. All in all, I have three full-length formals and one short one for winter, four good cashmere sweaters, twelve skirts, two school coats and lots of accessories. I wear mostly cotton dresses for school."

"Since we travel so much, I do my shopping through fashion magazines. I look over every issue of several magazines until I find what I want. Then I usually write to I. Magnin or Saks Fifth Avenue, to order from the picture. When I was in the States I got to know a buyer from each store and wrote directly to her. I love clothes so I *think* a lot about them and when I finally order something—it's just what I need and want."

Jody's tastes in clothes are simple but colorful. Her extremely slim figure makes all her clothes look graceful, she wears little make-up but pink lipstick, so her smooth hair, fresh face and very good manners give her a calm, Grace Kelly look. "I guess I am part military," she said with a laugh. "I *am* calm and I always get things done. One of my music teachers used to say, 'Get some temperament! Try shouting about something!' But I just don't."

However, in the midst of her hard-working, well-ordered young life, Jody does have a problem of sorts: "Jere and I have been dating for months and we graduated together. In the fall, I stay here to study and he is going back to the University of Colorado. His father is a sergeant here and my father has two more years at Nouasseur. It could be years before Jere and I see each other again.

"He was my prom date in June and we all had a wonderful evening. This time, living so close together on the base was an advantage. After the dance, everyone went home, changed into slacks and shirts and came back to my house. We let the boys run the kitchen and we all stayed up till five o'clock, with bacon, scrambled eggs and muffins. Such fun—and nobody's parents cared!"

Does Jody date anyone else beside Jere? "Well, sometimes. Once in a while I meet a nice boy in the church choir." (Colonel Regar is an Episcopalian, his wife was a Lutheran. When Jody first entered her teens, they decided on family unity and were all confirmed in the Episcopalian church in Yokahama, Japan).

"Also, one day I was driving four friends in our car and we were hit from behind by an army truck. Later, I dated the army lawyer who handled the case. But most of the girls in high school don't date the soldiers on the base. The reason is simple: there are so many soldiers, there just aren't enough girls to go around. It seems easier to date the teen-aged boys from school than get all involved. Some of the girls *do* date soldiers, but they usually get engaged or go steady.

"Something about today's teen-agers worries me," said Jody seriously. "I noticed it first back in Wilmington, North Carolina. Out of a class of six hundred, fifty got married right after graduation last year. I think by going steady and getting serious, teen-agers are bringing romance into their lives too early. This 'getting engaged' has become a trend.

"Jere—who is only eighteen now—was engaged to a girl in

the States before he came here. He had even given her an engagement ring and his family approved. He broke up with
her by mail and was miserable. After a while, I told him I
didn't want to hear any more of his troubles and we became
good friends. I don't want to become engaged until I'm
twenty-two or three and I wouldn't want to be married
before I was twenty-five." Then she laughed. "Maybe I've
just got Carnegie Hall on my mind."

Jody mentioned a second "problem" which she felt was
worrisome, but especially to the teen-agers at Nouasseur.
"There is just too much drinking here," she said, "and I
don't think either the grown-ups or the teens realize it.
Liquor can be bought on the base by the bottle, without the
usual U.S. liquor tax, so grown-ups can afford lots of parties.
And teen-agers just catch the mood. A Tom Collins costs
only thirty cents and we can get them when we order them.
I don't like to drink and can sip at a glass all night—but
some of my girl friends drink six in an evening! Sometimes
on dates we do go into the big hotels in town or little clubs,
like the Hatchet Club on the waterfront—and teens drink
whatever they want. At a big teen party at one of the clubs
right here on the base—round graduation time—grown-ups
kept sending bottles of champagne over to our table as "good
luck" gifts. I counted twenty bottles for a table of eight. Of
course, a lot of it got left—but the grown-ups don't seem to
think. Both Jere and I feel the same about this and, as I said,
I just nurse the same old drink along all night long. And I
don't feel that I'm less glamorous in anyone's mind for not
drinking!"

One thing about Jody seemed particularly "American":
her interest in and willingness to work. Throughout the

world, of course, there are teen-agers who slave from dawn to dark, simply for something to eat. On the other hand, many countries foster the attitude that wealthy, upper-class young people don't *have* to work—and shouldn't, especially girls. But Jody works because she wants to, because it forwards her education and because it interests her. And yet she doesn't sacrifice one moment of music, good manners or graceful living. For her, working is getting to know people.

Take the job she held for two summers, for instance: "In Harrisburg, Pennsylvania, my aunt, a widow, owns a combination gas station and twenty-room motel. I worked there, helping to take care of the place as a general receptionist, waitress and—at night—as a baby-sitter. It was hard work but such fun. I met wonderful people and some of them still write to me. One couple I am going to visit in Paris when I go up for the class reunion. And my favorites were two old Italian ladies who liked to listen to me play the violin. They light a candle in church every holy day for my success. My aunt has a touch of glamour in her thinking, and every few weeks she and I would fly into New York for the day, to see a play or go to a concert. And with all the tips I earned, I saved money besides."

Jody was very serious for a moment. "I don't know yet whether or not I am really a good violinist. Teachers say I am—but perhaps I'll only be a middling fiddler. I will still love music, though. Wherever I live, I'll be a part of the music of that country or that town. And most important of all," she said with a smile, "I'm enjoying life and my music myself."

[157]

10

FRANCINE ACH

France

A SOLEMN LITTLE GIRL stood with her mother watching the crowds shouting and pushing through the narrow streets of Lyon, France. It was June 6, 1945, the dramatic day that World War II ended in Europe. Out of the noise and confusion of that June afternoon, Francine Ach remembers one important thing: a big American soldier said, "I promised myself I'd kiss a French girl the day the war was over," and affectionately kissed the little child in front of her mother and the laughing crowd. Except for that kiss and a few clouded memories of distant planes in the sky, often American planes on their way to bomb German-held targets in France, Francine has no clear memories of the war.

But to her parents, the long war years were "a sad and fearful time." And they seem constantly trying to make up to Francine for those years, giving her all the things *now* they had meant to give her all her life.

At seventeen, a Parisian teen-ager now, Francine is a pretty, pampered and petted girl, with a social life, friends and wardrobe that teens all over the world might envy. But, as a balance, she has a serious streak to her nature, and the rigid demands of French school life set standards and schedules that leave her little time to herself. Her play-girl-student schedule is exhausting. No wonder Madame Ach says with fondness—and a willingness to pay all the bills— "Poor Francine! After her studies, she deserves any vacation she can get. Sometimes at the end of the day she is quite pale."

Francine's school, Le Lycee Jean de la Fontaine, is a big modern building, four stories high and nearly half a block square, standing in "the green belt," a wealthy section of Paris distinguished for its parks and fresh shrubbery. Francine Ach is one of 1800 girls from ten to eighteen who arrive promptly for half-past eight classes each morning, loaded with books, faces scrubbed of make-up and with neat school smocks of pale beige cotton folded over their arms. Many of the girls come by bicycle, whizzing expertly through the crowded Paris streets like giant insects, but Francine walks the few blocks from the new apartment building which is now her home.

Each school day is much the same for Francine: up at seven o'clock, rush for the first class, a lunch break from eleven-thirty until two, then classes until five or six o'clock. On Thursdays, French students have no school at all but they go to classes on Saturday until half past twelve. ("It's done that way to give the parents at least a half day by themselves without the children hanging about," explains Francine practically.)

After school, Francine may walk home with a friend or two, perhaps even stop at someone's apartment for a cup of chocolate and a few minutes chatter. But never would a student from the Lycee stop at one of the many sidewalk cafes so popular in France. There are no drugstores with soda fountains, no favorite sandwich shops, no "high school hangouts" for after-school relaxation. Aside from the big gray school itself, there is no sign that nearly 2000 young people spend most of their days in that neighborhood. There are, in fact, no after-school clubs, sports meets, dramatic rehearsals—no class plays, sororities, school newspapers or school dances. It is a school for "book learning" only. On most days, Francine walks straight home, to crowd in as much studying as possible before dinner. Higher school in Paris is a serious, even somber, business, without the fun and gay trimmings that American schools consider a part of education and individual development.

The eight-o'clock evening meal is a welcome break in Francine's long day. The French have always been famous for their excellent cooking and interest in food, and though Francine is a willowy 110 pounds for her 5 feet, 6 inches, she has a big, typically teen-aged appetite. Dinnertime at the Achs', as in most French families, is a leisurely family time. The dining room opens right off the living room, where the radio is probably playing softly, Monsieur Ach is usually home from the office to take his place at the head of the table. (Monsieur Ach is a sales distributor for a large bottled-gas firm, selling throughout France.) Andre, Francine's only brother, a sophisticated twenty-six-year-old who works for an import company and lives alone in a small hotel, has dinner with his family once or twice a week. The overhead chandeliers shine out over the giant, carved open-front chests, crowded with china and silver, that Madame Ach inherited from her parents. (Francine says candidly, "I hope they all get lost before it's my turn to get them.") They also shine out over the packing boxes, still standing in one corner, and light up a generous evening meal. The menu will probably be something as substantial as hot watercress soup, cold sliced ham, eggs, jam, perhaps cold fish with mayonnaise and, for dessert, a piece of good French cheese and fresh fruit. Though wine is certainly more popular than water in France, the Achs rarely drink it with their meals, and a bottle is brought to the table only on special occasions. The maid serves dinner, a white apron tied on over the sweater and skirt, her cloth slippers shuffling over the new parquet floors. The atmosphere is homey and pleasant, comfortable without any touch of formality.

Mme. Ach is a chic, humorous woman who works with her husband, soliciting orders by telephone from home for his bottled-gas agency. ("Naturally," she said with a smile, "if I went out to business, I would have to get this white hair dyed blonde again.") The maid, herself a teen-ager, just in from the country, cares for the apartment, goes to market, does the cooking and laundry and has a little room of her own in the basement, with other maids from the building, for wages of about fifteen dollars a week.

After dinner, Francine, who never helps with the housework, hurries to her room for a couple of hours of study before bedtime. There is little furniture there at the moment, just a wooden wardrobe, a chair and desk with a lamp and a narrow bed. But the Achs have lived in their new apartment for just one month and the furniture will have to come a piece at a time. They realize how lucky they are to have found a new three-bedroom, two-bath apartment in beautiful but old, overcrowded and very expensive Paris. Except for the war years (then the family moved to rural Lyon where Madame Ach worked in a munitions factory and Monsieur Ach, demobilized from the French army, made a sketchy living selling cutlery), Francine has lived most of her life in a small, groundfloor apartment on one of the crooked little streets on the Left Bank. The building was of crumbling gray stone, dark and damp and over two hundred years old, without central heating and with limited electricity, picturesque but exceedingly uncomfortable. So eager were the Achs to live in the new apartment that they moved in even before the building was finished. The front entrance is still heaped with tiles and dusty bags of cement, hallways are without lights and some of the walls in the interior building are merely stretches of unplastered lathing. In about a year, the completed building will be as modern and attractive as any good apartment building in a large American city. And from Francine's bedroom, high on the seventh floor, the big plate glass window looks out over Paris, with a clear view of the delicate Eiffel Tower and the distant white dome of the Church of the Sacred Heart. But such living is expensive in Paris. To buy this apartment, the Achs were forced to pay nearly twenty-five thousand dollars in cash and a monthly maintenance fee of about fifty-four dollars.

Because of high construction costs, rent control of old buildings and the general up-and-down conditions after the war, housing in Paris, one of the most glamorous cities of the world, is among the worst in Europe. The average age of the buildings is about eighty-three years and one-quarter of all apartments have no running water. Housewives manage with jugs of water carried from pumps in the streets, sometimes a down-and-up walk of six flights, on narrow, dark staircases.

Among the rural population of France, about twenty million people, only a third have running water in their homes. Twenty-five per cent of all couples married in 1948 are still looking for homes of their own. These young people may live with their parents or in hotel rooms or in single rooms without kitchens. In fact, it is to this "one room with cooking" group that Mr. Ach's very prosperous bottled gas company sells much of its product. Therefore, in spite of the great expense involved, the Achs are enjoying their luck in having found a new and roomy apartment.

Because Le Lycee Jean de la Fontaine is in a wealthy section of the big city, most of Francine's classmates are of the same social and economic group and as "lucky" as she. Her weekly allowance of $2.25 is about average and her school wardrobe of six sweaters, two straight skirts and three jersey dresses is much like that of the other girls. No make-up is allowed in this all-girl school (though a little light lipstick is overlooked by the faculty for the seventeen- and eighteen-year olds), and, with their short Leslie Caron haircuts or long, sleek ponytails, many of the girls look like young, hard-working ballet dancers. But the atmosphere of the school is that of a university. The single bulletin board in the main hall carries only terse announcements of when classes will meet and such notices as: "All students wishing to take extra courses in Swedish, Danish or Vietnamese report to Room 220." In the classrooms, the female professor lectures, often from a single map hung on the wall, while the students—thirty to fifty in a class—take notes. The classroom equipment is simple, usually long tables, with a comfortable chair for each student. Francine's current program is a heavy one: World History, Geography, Physics, 18th-19th Century French literature, English literature and language, Spanish and two hours of gymnastics per week. She also tries to do "outside reading" and keeps a little notebook listing authors whose books she has read, including Saroyan, Hemingway and Faulkner, as well as French writers.

During World War II, when the Germans occupied Paris from 1940 to 1944, this school was used as a barracks for German soldiers and much of the school's equipment was lost or damaged. Teachers still point with annoyance to broken walls or damaged fixtures in the lavatories which they insist are souvenirs of the Germans. Slowly, a little each year, equipment is being replaced in the chemistry lab and library shelves are filling. Bitterness against their German neighbors, who invaded France twice in a period of less than thirty years, is strong among the French. Even teen-agers such as Francine, who was very small during World

War II, see constant reminders on Paris street corners: small stone placques on buildings, sometimes with a candle or flowers and some such message as "In Memory of Jacques Croix, age 18. Shot on this spot June 10th, 1944, a victim of the Germans."

One of the most pleasant spots in Francine's school is the lunchroom, a huge, brightly lighted room where about three hundred students may eat at one time. The students are served "family style" at long tables for eight, with napkins and tablecloths in fresh pink and blue check. On each table is an ornate tile hot-plate to hold the main dish. This is passed hand to hand. There are two loaves of long, crisp French bread per eight persons and a two-quart bottle of beer on the table for those who want it. On a typical day, the students may eat as much as they wish of chilled vegetables with mayonnaise, sliced pork roast with buttered Brussels sprouts, a green salad and cake with cream for dessert for about forty cents each. The tables are served by university students, who rush over to help out for seventy-five cents a day and their own execellent lunch.

For Francine, and all her friends in this second to last year at the Lycee, life is overshadowed by the huge scholastic bugabear of all French students: *le bachot. Le bachot* is short for the French word for *baccalaureat,* the equivalent of the U.S. college board exams, and it determines whether or not a student is eligible for entrance to the universities. The tests, which take about two days each, are given in two sections, the first when the students are sixteen or seventeen and the second, the following year. Out of the 130,000 students who take the tests each year, only about sixty-five per cent will be able to pass. In the meantime, pupils cram and worry over such tough questions as: "Many writers have experienced and enjoyed solitude. Have you? In any case, try to determine very sincerely what you feel in a moment of solitude and illustrate your analysis with experiences of Montagne, Descartes, Chateaubriand, Pascal, La Fontaine, Rousseau, Lamartine, etc."

The tensions over *le bachot* are so great that all Paris breaks loose in celebration the day they are over. Last year, about three thousand students gathered in one spot, across from the Cathedral of Notre Dame, to mill through the city streets, overturn the little French cars and pelt passers-by with sacks of flour and fish. The celebration was so violent that sixty students were arrested and several policemen needed hospitalization. Even though she doesn't take her first *bachot* until this year, Francine joined last year's crowd along the Boulevard Saint Germaine de Pres, singing and tagging onto the end of a snake dance.

With school life so difficult at one extreme, Francine's "holiday life" swings to the other for extravagant, storybook gaiety. Besides the summer vacation from July to September, she has ten free days at Christmastime and two weeks at Eastertime. This Christmas vacation, just as she has since she was eleven years old, Francine took a week-long skiing holiday in Austria, traveling with a chaperoned group of skiers, ranging from seventeen to thirty years old to a little town high in the Austrian Alps. The trip cost about eighty-five dollars and Francine had a small room to herself in the ski lodge. The days were spent skiing, with lunch on the mountaintop, tea at the lodge around five, dinner late in the evening and dancing around the fire until about two in the morning. (Francine packed a scoop-necked sweater in black cashmere and a pair of tightly pegged black and blue striped toreador trousers for "ski dancing.") On New Year's Eve, a record evening of fun for Francine, the crowd danced until three o'clock, stopped for a lunch of cakes, sandwiches, gin and schnapps, bought in the village earlier in the day, and then danced till dawn. "All the girls had a wonderful time," Francine says happily, "because three-fourths of the party were boys."

Francine, who is not only pretty but has a manner both gay and gentle, has always been popular, though she was not allowed to go to parties with boys until she was seventeen. During the last skiing holiday, she became very fond of a tall, dark-haired psychiatry student of nineteen and he was her chief "flirt" on the trip. ("Flirt" can mean anything from "special interest" to "steady date.") But her new apartment has no telephone—phones are almost as difficult to get as apartments—so she did not hear from him again after both returned to Paris.

During her dating life, Francine has had five "flirts," boys she has gone out with at least several times. Parties at home are the favorite date activity with her crowd, usually dancing to records, with cakes and soft drinks as refreshments, though frequently some of the older boys bring a bottle of gin for themselves. Francine herself does not drink but she admits that occasional boys set out "to get drunk just for the fun of it." On her vacations, she has sometimes met American soldiers and she has the impression that Americans often drink too much. On the recent Christmas vacation, Francine and a girl friend asked two American soldiers at the ski lodge, "Why are you drinking so much tonight?"

The men answered, "Because our wives are back home and

we're lonesome." With a sophisticated shrug, Francine concedes she thinks that a most reasonable answer.

"When we go to parties here, we stay out very late," she explains, "but it is the custom. Almost no boy ever has a car, so we go everywhere by subway or bus. I usually get home at two or three o'clock in the morning, especially if we go to a party in the suburbs." Once Francine and a date missed the last late-night subway and couldn't catch one till six the next morning ("we just went back to the party and danced") but that time her parents were both worried and angry. Though she considers her family good-natured and generous, Francine also considers them strict. "They must always know exactly where I am going, must meet the boy first—everything."

For the over-twenty crowd in Paris, a visit to a "cave," a tiny, inexpensive night club with a small jazz band or piano player, is considered a favorite date. Most young Parisians are jazz mad and when Louis Armstrong came to town to give a series of concerts, even Madame Ach joined the theater mob.

Away from the smock uniform of school, the Parisian teen has little time for clothes fads or slang. For a while, pony-tails were a "must" hairdo and after school hours girls favored black skirts with black high-necked sweaters, worn with a single, heavy medal (just costume jewelry) hung round the neck on a chain. In slang, a good-looking girl might be simply a "nice doll" and a handsome boy would warrant the compliment "he's from thunder!." "I'm dry!" is a much-used phrase, expressing everything from boredom to being unable to answer a question in class. And the telephone, for reasons Francine could not explain, is referred to

by teens simply as "the bigaphone." Movies are, of course,
a teen favorite in Paris, and Francine usually goes at least
one night a week, often with her mother. *The Moon Is Blue*
and *Singing in the Rain* were American favorites and often,
around her own neighborhood, she sees such oldies as *I
Married a Witch,* with Veronica Lake and Frederic March.
Francine said she had never heard an Eddie Fisher record
but knew all about Marlon Brando. "But not from his
movies," she declared. "He had a romance with a French
girl and, of course, we all love to read about a romance!"

Francine's parents treat her always with an indulgent
gaiety, as if she is a pretty and valuable decoration to their
lives. She studies hard and they, in turn, give her all the
love and material props they can to keep her life pleasant.
As a family, they have taken many exciting vacations together—in the south of France, Italy, Spain and England.
Except for the war years, the family picture album is crowded
with snapshots of Andre and Francine in vacation spots. But,
unlike American custom, the highlights of Francine's life
now are the vacations she takes alone. Besides the ski trips,
she has lived with families in the south of France and in
England, the latter trips made to perfect her English, which
she has studied for six years. For one month last summer, an
English girl stayed with the Achs in Paris, while Francine
visited *her* home in England. But in all her traveling, Francine has never gone to Germany. The country does not
attract her, even though it is only a few hours of travel away.

France itself is a proud and beautiful country, small
enough to give all Frenchmen a national sameness and big
enough to support a span of life from the ultra-chic existence
of Paris to the simple peasant living of the farm and coastal

fishing villages. Paris itself is a queen city, a huge but grace-ful sprawl of buildings, ranging from the Cathedral of Notre Dame and the splendid Louvre Museum, which covers several city blocks, to the sidewalk cafés and the rickety, picturesque buildings that climb the crooked streets of Montmartre, in the old artists' section of town. Paris draws world respect as an art and fashion center, students crowd from every country to the Sorbonne University and tourists jam every hotel the year around, to walk along the Boulevard Champs Elysee, eat pressed duck at the Tour d'Argent and watch the gray River Seine in the twilight. At the bustling Mediterranean port city of Marseille, the docks are busy with freighters; the Cote d'Azur strip of southern France is famous for such luxury vacation towns as Nice, Cannes and Juan les Pins. Up from Bordeaux, going north, the fields are lined with the stubby grapevines that have made French wine labels choice for centuries; in the Loire valley still stand the big, stately chateaux where the dukes of France lived and ruled in feudal times. Orleans, Limoge and Lyon are booming manufacturing towns; the airline, Air France, boasts the longest transport routes of any line on earth. In short, France has a little of everything—historic splendor and modern industry, thatch-roof peasant cottages on country lanes and bright gas stations and quick lunch diners along the busy main highways. But in the years since World War II, France has been a troubled nation: the cost of living has soared, membership in the Communist Party has increased, the colony of Syria was lost, and such French colonies as Morocco and Algeria—from which the nation drew both revenue and prestige—have been, respectively, given inde-pendence and is seeking it. The premiership of the nation has changed hands a dozen times. Especially for young people, France is now a country of uncertainty and unrest, with the hopes for the future not so brilliant as the record of the past.

But Francine insists that "politics don't touch me" and confines her newspaper reading to sports, fashions and "murder news." But she is very proud of France, neverthless, and quite certain that Paris is the most chic city in the world. The United States, she believes, has "a more comfortable life, more machines to help women do things, more wealth— but the people are not very serious." Francine herself is a charming combination of the "gay" and the "serious" in life—but when she is serious, she does not know just what to be serious about. The future, for instance, is a serious but vague problem to her. In France, all pupils come to a dividing point educationally at the age of ten—and go one of two ways: those who qualify scholastically and financially will go to a school such as the Lycee and then on to a university; the others will go into trade schools and the manual arts. However, there are many government scholarships to help poor but good students who want to continue with "higher education." Francine, as a privileged Lycee student, studies hard every book put in front of her—but she has no idea what she would like to do when she is out of school.

In her country, except in the arts or professions, there are not many good jobs for women—and salaries are usually low. A primary schoolteacher, for instance, would earn about eighty-five dollars a month, with three hundred dollars the salary for a full-fledged professor. A typist might earn about sixty dollars a month, and a typist with two languages about seventy-five dollars. Wages for clerking in the small shops (and in Paris the majority of shops are small, family-owned affairs, with only two super-markets and a few major department stores) are as low as fifty dollars a month. There is another problem. As one of the teachers explained it, "We still have strong class consciousness here. Most girls from the wealthier upper classes would not take a secretarial job at all unless it was with their father's company. Girls still do not have the tradition of "working."

Francine, of course, is not typical of every girl in France, just as a single girl from New York City would not represent in every way every teen-aged girl in our nation. But Francine has her own story, and her story is much like that of most girls of her age and income group living in Paris.

What will she do with her life until she reaches twenty-three or twenty-four, the age at which she thinks she would like to marry? Francine just shrugs and smiles. Undoubtedly she will keep herself very busy for, even now, one of her favorite expressions (and a favorite expression in all France) is: "I have no time." When she does marry, her demands for a husband will be romantic and simple: "I would like him to be sympathetic and with a good character. I do not care if he is in commercial business or the professions. But I like boys who are nice, gay and teasing. Size makes no difference but he should be a good dancer. I would like him to be nice to me and my children—I think I would like three because we French like children. And perhaps," she added with a hopeful smile, "he will even help me cook." (To help around the house in any way at all is very rare for a European male.) "I know nothing about money," Francine admits, "but I think we could start on $150 or $180 a month for everything."

In the meantime, there are long days at school, *le bachot* to work for, the holidays to dream about. Recently, the French writer, André Maurois, discussed girl students in Paris. He wrote, "What strikes me most about those girls is their courage. They don't ask themselves if life has any meaning: they live it." Francine Ach is like that.

11

IDOWU SOMNYIWA

Nigeria, West Africa

IT WAS A DAMP, gray afternoon when I first met Idowu
Somnyiwa, and the air was heavy with midsummer African heat. He stood tracing patterns in the dust with his bare
brown toes as we talked, his face—soft and rounded as a
child's—damp with nervousness. Behind him the monster
blossoms of a giant red canna lily stood higher than his head,

swaying in the stiff wind that blew in from the Atlantic. The breeze smelled of fish and sea moisture. Here in Lagos, Nigeria, on the west coast of Africa, a torrential summer rain was about to break loose for the third time that day.

"I am eighteen," said Idowu in soft, shy English, thinking hard before every word. "I must be eighteen because I went to primary school in my town for nine years." This young Nigerian was born in a straw-hut village, far outside Lagos, and no records were kept for him or three brothers and a sister, though he says his mother tried to remember the years by the seasons and the feast days. Standing in his brief khaki shorts and white sport shirt, Idowu seemed boyish and immature, no more than fifteen years old, and a very small part of this bustling city.

"My mother is dead now," he explained, "and so is my father. But I am sure I must be eighteen. Anyway," he added brightly, "I am younger than my older brother and he is thirty."

Idowu lives with his brother, his brother's wife and their infant child in a squalid, two-room, clapboard house on noisy, crowded Bambose Street, in Lagos. All day long high native music or soothing British dance tunes, interspersed with the scores of British soccer games played in far-off England, blare out from radios in the tiny houses. Children play happily in the narrow, dusty street, avoiding the flowing open gutters that carry household garbage and human waste out to the sea. At night, the dim street is lit by the wavering glow of string wicks floating in tins of palm oil and voices and laughter sound from the crowded rooms long after midnight.

Some of the worst slums in the world exist in the heart of Lagos; in one section 28,000 people are jammed into sixty

[175]

acres and a few homes are just roofed passageways, open to the street on both ends. Because living conditions are cramped, people are out of their houses at the first light of dawn and spend most of the day on the streets. Idowu and his family, for instance, sleep four to a room and a visiting relative is never turned away. Other families are even more crowded. Thousands of Nigerians have moved into town from the countryside, looking for employment, till even a doorway is a choice place to curl up in for the night.

By day and by night, Lagos—the capital of Nigeria as Washington is the capital of the United States—is like an outsized ant village populated by people, human ants frantically alive with noise, color and smell. There is movement on all sides, taxis, bicycles and foot passengers, a constant streaming of brightly dressed, heavily burdened Nigerians coming and going in the chores of city life. People are everywhere, their long cotton garments, mostly prints in shades of blue, lighting the drab city streets like a growth of cornflowers. Sometimes the numbers of people and the bustle seem more than the eye can encompass; looking over the central market place is like looking at a drop of water through a microscope, with movement and life by the thousands.

Nigeria itself is a large country (370,000 square miles) with more people than any other single country in Africa and a larger population than, for instance, Spain. But compared to the vastness of all Africa, it is small—no more than a thumb folded over the palm of a big man's left hand. Into Lagos a quarter of a million people have jammed, living occasionally in two-story, cement-block houses but much more frequently in the rundown slum areas. They include Hausas, Ibos, Yorubas, the three leading tribes, and members of over

200 other tribes, all Nigerians but each observing the individual customs, traditions and language of his own tribe,
with most speaking as well the English language of the
British colonizers who have controlled this country since
1914.

Coastal Nigeria also has a close, warm link with the United
States. In the slave days, this area was one of the chief sources
for the pathetic human cargo that found its way, chained,
starved and beaten, to American shores. In the 1780's, as
many as 100,000 Negroes a year were transported across the
Atlantic and almost all of the 15,000,000 Negroes now United
States citizens had their origins in Africa's West Coast. It
was not only white slave traders who were responsible for
this inhuman practice; it took the cooperation of local chiefs
to capture and sell their countrymen and it was not until
1901 that slavery was declared illegal within the boundaries
of Nigeria itself.

Just as all Africa is not like Nigeria, so all Nigeria is not
just like Lagos—but then Lagos is the most sophisticated,
prosperous town and the seat of the government. It is also
Idowu Somnyiwa's new home.

"I will be a primary schoolteacher some day," he said
proudly. "My brother is helping me. Each day he goes to
his store in town, where he sells machines—typewriters,
weighing machines, parts of things—and I stay in the house
and study my books."

(Mr. Somnyiwa's store is a dark, eight-by-ten-foot cubicle
with only one opening, a raisable, corrugated metal door,
flush with the street, to let in both light and air. He special-
izes in locks and chains, with a large stock of pedals, handle-
bars and bicycle parts. His day is long—from eight in the

[177]

morning until whatever hour the last customer has ceased to look at his merchandise, haggle over price or simply stop to chat. Then Mr. Somnyiwa snuffs out the palm oil pots that light his merchandise, padlocks the metal door and peddles off on his bicycle to the two rooms on Bambose Street).

"Every day," explained Idowu, "I listen to the English lessons on the radio. From nine to ten in the morning, I study arithmetic. From one to two, I teach myself typing and shorthand. In the fall, I will take an examination to try to get into a higher school for four years.

"After that, I will be a teacher. I will find myself a village school and teach there. I want to do something to help my people."

In that short speech, young Idowu had touched on two important things characteristic of life in most parts of Nigeria:

First is the fact that his older brother was helping him to get an education. In this country, family feeling—based on the old unity of tribe and village, is very strong; it is traditional to live closely and help one's family. Immediately after his parents' death, Idowu was taken in by cousins, in the rambling town of Abeokuta, some miles from Lagos. As soon as his older brother, his nearest blood kin, had a home of his own, the boy came to live with him. In every village or town, the local chief will have a bigger, more lavish house, and around him, like ripples in a pond, will range the smaller houses or huts of relatives, right out to the most distant cousin. A Nigerian family wealthy enough to entertain rarely gives a feast for guests outside the family circle. Both living and "spirit" members of any family are kept close, and country roads and clearings around the villages are dotted with little shrines to the family dead. In fact, in many country areas it is still customary to bury dead members of the family right under the floor of the main room of the house. So it is completely in keeping with tradition for the older Somnyiwa to watch over his younger brother.

The second characteristic attitude is Idowu's intense interest in "getting an education." Millions of Nigerians are content to remain illiterate and many of the most successful merchants and traders can neither read nor write (in fact, this is true of about ninety-five per cent of the population) but with those who are interested in an education, the desire seems to burn like a fever. In Lagos, there are many public schools and in the miles immediately outside town, mission schools, set in clearings cut into the heavy bush, are as frequent as gasoline stations in California.

Education to a Nigerian can mean many things besides the satisfaction that comes from knowledge—higher income, social standing, a better life, a chance to work as something besides servant or laborer under the British. In Lagos, the yen for learning shows itself in many small ways. Politicians list their school degrees like trophies, newspapers are written in flowery, extra-erudite language, with no two-syllable word ever used when a five-syllable one can be found. Even the beauty columns are written in language as sententious as an editorial in the *New York Times*. In hotels, restaurants and even along the streets, children or young people stop strangers with the plea, "Help me be dentist!" or "Help me be lawyer!"; marriage-age young women consider as prizes the "been-tos," those male students who have been to England or America to study. In one Lagos book store, a shelf in-

[179]

cluded all available "how to do it" books, including the title, *How to Stop Smoking*.

Out in the bush country, families or whole villages may chip in to send a bright boy into Lagos to school or even to a foreign university. (One enterprising college graduate, educated in Pennsylvania, returned to Nigeria and made a brisk living selling phoney scholarships to schools in the United States. However, he is now doing his post-graduate work in a Nigerian jail!) As far back as the 1700's, a few boys went to London to study, yet today only about 20,000 of all Nigerians have the equivalent of a secondary education.

In a country which is developing in leaps and bounds, education sometimes behaves in the same way, with students desiring high degrees before they actually have enough education to get out of sixth grade. On the other hand, good students—eager to make the most of opportunity—often earn top marks in universities, learn several languages and qualify for several degrees. At the moment, there is still too much "higher education"—young students aiming for fields such as medicine, law and teaching, with not enough in-betweens to fill the great need for engineers, veterinarians, dieticians—and automobile mechanics. But Nigeria now has enough education to make it determined to have more.

In Idowu's present life in Lagos, his bare feet beat a very small circle—his brother's home, his brother's shop, church, occasional visits to the market place—and back home. A trip to the market, where he sometimes goes to shop for his sister-in-law, is like an hour or two at a carnival. The noise of bargaining, shouting, hawking, the color of open trays of food and bolts of bright cloth, the smells of fried fish, spices and damp waste running in every gutter fills the air.

The main market place is in the center of town, a primitive, open-air collection of ramshackle tin-roof stalls, running in lines according to merchandise and covering about four blocks. Lagos is an island city, surrounded by lagoons and the long waves of the Atlantic. At night, the market place is deserted. As the first light of dawn silhouettes the fringe of palm trees around the square, people begin to stream into the market place to set up shop. Nigerians are head-carriers when on foot and often when riding bicycles. Women balance immense loads, wrapped in cloth and sometimes set on big, woven-grass trays. In the early light, bicycles, bare feet and pullcarts pour toward the market place like sand through a funnel.

Traditionally, most of the sellers are women, dubbed "market mammies," who sit all day shouting out their wares. These are not shy, awkward bush-country women; many are shrewd, calculating businesswomen, with heads as busy as adding machines. A few of the most prosperous traders buy goods in town on charge account, sell the merchandise in outlying villages or distant bush markets at a great profit, keeping the complicated arithmetic in their heads and sending a constant flow of goods traveling into the most remote areas. Padlocks, alarm clocks, wristwatches, razor blades and sunglasses are especially popular off-beat products. Fish is sold, and a little meat, plus flour stuffs, flat baskets of yams, greenleaf and other vegetables—but the most colorful booths are for spices, jewelry and cloth.

The spices, often sold by the teaspoonful, range from white alum to powdered yellow saffron, twisted dried roots and dusky orange curry powder, all set out on small trays to be bought and carried away in twists of newspaper or big leaves.

All of the jewelry is of a poor quality, bright psuedo-gold ear-rings and bracelets and tray after tray of glass beads, brilliant and symmetrical as berries. In the cosmetic stalls are sold powdered antimony for eye-shadow, a ruddy paste for the lips and powdered chalk, chiefly in dusky yellow and bright blue, to be used as a face powder, plus many other beautifiers, powders and ungents unfamiliar to our dressing tables.

The cloth booths, which occupy a block by themselves, are always crowded with customers, since the most popular Nigerian dress is a simple, bright cotton garment made from cloth manufactured in England. Men and women alike wear a loose, smocklike garment with long, wide sleeves. It is cool and easy to keep fresh in the muggy climate. Sometimes men wear the garment in plain white, but most frequently the choice for both sexes is an all-over print of fishes, elephants, stripes, circles or just sunburst designs, and sometimes a little of each in one print. Also popular is fabric printed with the portrait of Queen Elizabeth of England, sometimes coupled with a picture of her husband, The Duke of Edinburgh, with the ratio about three queen's heads to one duke. The cloth, a bit stiff and smelling strongly of dye, flutters around the fabric booths like exotic flags. Almost everyone wears a head-covering—cotton turbans for the women, tied low over the eyebrows and butterfly-bowed in back and, for men, flat-topped skullcaps in striped velvet. Many pampered babies bob along on their mothers' backs, wearing tiny bonnets of wooly chenile tufts to protect their heads from the sun.

As brilliant as the cloth are the displays of tinware and plastics, with everything from combs to pails in pastel plastic and colorful enamelware pots and basins spread over the counters and sidewalks. I noticed one particularly striking

[182]

white enamelled tray, printed with bright geraniums and two doves, one white and one dark-feathered, holding a ribbon between them bearing the word "peace." This, plus most of the tinware, had come from Japan. During one of the summer cloudbursts, I listened as the rain beat down on the unprotected hardware and the ping, bang, rattle and swoosh had the frantic musical effect of a Spike Jones arrangement.

Prominent and busy were the witchcraft or "juju" booths, littered with bits and things for making special spells and magic potions. Rather than something touched with horror or mystery, they looked more like drab, weather-worn heaps in some backwoods dump. Most of the articles seemed dried, wizened and—to me—unrecognizable, though I could distinguish monkeys' skulls, dogs' ears, little paws, snake fangs and the dried-grape eyes of some animal. At one booth I asked about the use of a pair of crow's wings and the young male clerk explained that they were to be burned, the ashes mixed with rancid cow's butter and applied to the forehead to cure headache. This, of course, was not meant to be "magic" but "medicine."

Lagos—and all of Nigeria—is a land of contrasts, as if civilization had no more than scuffed a few bare spots on the thick green surface of the land. What has already been done is impressive; what remains to be done is, to the eyes of a stranger, staggering. For instance, superstitions, fears and witchcraft practices in some parts of the country seem as primitive, as savage as they were centuries ago, when medicine men ruled the villages. During my visit, a young Nigerian clergyman had the misfortune to hit a child with his car in a village not too far inland and he was promptly torn to pieces by the villagers! Yet in Lagos—and even more impressively in Ibadan, many miles inland—there are hospitals with equipment and skills to match any in the world. A new university was founded in Ibadan in 1948, with a library of 100,000 books. Again, to some Nigerians, a bicycle is the height of wealth and luxury; other millions have traveled no more than a long footwalk outside the home village (in some remote areas, no white man has ever been seen). Yet hundreds of Nigerians think nothing of traveling by air in huge, modern British planes that link several of the major cities and make forty flights per day outside the country. A wayside market may consist of nothing more than three women, some baskets of merchandise and a hollow on the roadside, yet in Lagos there is a modern, three-story department store (British-operated) that sells everything from current best sellers to electrical equipment and Max Factor pancake make-up in dark brown. And every bit and piece is an important part of the changing jigsaw puzzle picture.

Idowu's market trips are usually simple ones; to buy a bit of spice, some thread, a daub of flour paste or some dried fish. He has no money of his own and still seems surprised that his brother has anything to spend.

"But we eat well," he explained, pausing as if to think a moment about what he had had to eat recently. "For breakfast, we have porridge and tea, at lunch time we have tea and bread and in the evening we have tea and rice. Sometimes we have fish with rice and sometimes a little meat on feast days."

(I stopped one afternoon in a tiny Nigerian fishing village on a creek bank. In front of every second straw hut, a woman or girl was pounding out the evening meal, using a pestle with a four-foot handle to grind the meal in a big wooden bowl resting on the ground. The meal was made up of dried corn, rice and beans—all to be mixed with river water and eaten warmed up. On the low roofs of the houses lay rows of fish, scaled and split open, drying in the late afternoon sun.

On another occasion we paused to talk with two women shoppers, trudging a weary nine miles from town out to their villages in the bush. One showed me her purchases, carried in a tin basin on her head—an unwrapped bone that looked like a mutton knuckle with a few ounces of meat on it, a paper of saffron, some rice, two dozen kola nuts and a package of yellow and orange beads. Not much there for a quick casserole; but, of course, villagers can depend on yams and a few greenstuffs from their own gardens.

In the northern town of Kano, we watched big-muscled laborers loading huge sacks of groundnuts (peanuts) on freight cars, moving hour after hour in rhythmic rows. Clay jugs of water stood nearby but no lunch pails. These men sustained themselves for the whole day on a handful or two of peanuts. It is fortunate they can live on so little, for wages here were even lower than in Lagos: about one dollar a week for work on the farms, $1.25 a week for work in the perfume factories and wages ranging upward from fifty-six cents a day for more skilled work.)

A curiosity in all parts of Nigeria is the use of the kola nut as a stimulant. This nut, about the size, shape and color of a tulip bulb, is sold everywhere and it is nibbled at as an assuager of appetite and a nerve stimulant. Around the streets, these nuts are peddled as we might sell hot peanuts at a circus and every market place has them for sale by the trayful. I spent an entire day with a young Nigerian who ate and drank nothing at all except the frequent nibbles from the kola nut carried in his shirt pocket. To me, they *tasted* like fresh tulip bulbs, too—crisp, hard and bitter and with no "lift" at all. But many Nigerians almost live on them.

Idowu seems sturdy, though a little slow and with low energy. "I like games," he assured me. "After my studies each day, I go out into the yard to kick football with my friends. And I like running games. I like to race."

By religion, Idowu and his family are Anglicans. His mother and father were converted in their village when he was a little boy and he is an ardent churchgoer. "Besides studying the Bible at the house every evening, I go to services every Sunday," he said. "And once a month I go to a church party. There are mostly older women there but we pray and discuss the progress of the church."

In this coastal area of Nigeria, most of the conventionally religious people are Christians but in the North, where the Hausa tribes predominate, the Moslem religion is stronger. These religious differences, as well as distance and varying tribal customs and dialects, split the unity of the country. The Moslems, according to their religious traditions, have changed the close companionship of village life, keep their women veiled, often take up to three wives and usually prefer a secluded family life behind high walls, to keep the women folk segregated. This practice interferes, too, with the Nigerian government's aim for more general public education, since most Moslems prefer not to educate the young girls in school.

But Idowu has never been to the northern section of his country. In fact, even in imagination, his views are small. Though there are several theaters in Lagos, he has never been to a movie and his whole idea of the world comes from the few miles he has traveled into bush country, and from books and local newspapers.

"Some of my friends have gone to movies," he explained simply, "but I have no money. I listen to good African music on the radio and I go to church. And I visit with friends and my family."

But many other teen-agers do go to the small outdoor theaters, situated in walled-in backyards off the main streets, whenever they can get the few cents asked for admission. Folding chairs are arranged under the open skies, with a strip of roofing over the back few rows for those who can pay an extra ten cents and the first movie starts around nine o'clock, or as soon as night gives the screen a dark enough backdrop.

Musicals are always popular, British or American, with Randolph Scott westerns the top favorite and science fiction or horror movies running a close second in popularity. "Most of us get our information about America from the movies," one teen-aged boy explained with a laugh. "So you will pardon us if we think of you as all tough or all luxury."

It was interesting to note that the ads run on the screen before the feature picture—advertisements for cars, beauty products, anti-malaria tablets, etc.—all used Nigerian models and Nigerian locale. Even the shining new cars were photographed on pot-holed country roads; this is Nigeria and the emphasis is clearly on the Nigerians, not the British. Nigeria became a British colony in 1914, and the rule was firm; however, since 1947, many changes have been made and the government is now principally in the hands of the Nigerians. By 1958—if unity can be obtained throughout the country—it is hoped that Nigeria will become independent and a member, of the British Commonwealth. At the moment, there is great agitation for "freedom now" but little rancor against the British; the great day of freedom will probably be celebrated on schedule—and with good will on both sides. However, it did seem incongruous, sitting with Nigerians under the dark Nigerian sky, to see every movie end with a brief colored film of Queen Elizabeth of England, on horseback and regally uniformed, while the night air rang with the strains of God Save the Queen.

Dancing, too, is popular in Lagos but outside the pocketbook and tastes of a shy boy like Idowu. In the villages and back country, dances are community affairs, with families, young and old, joining in. In town, dancing is most popular with younger people and Saturday night the dance spots are crowded.

We joined a group one evening in the back garden of a small, edge-of-town hotel. The five-piece band, called "The West End Cool Cats," beat out "hi-life" music, a loud, danceable rhythm currently popular, and the couples, mostly in their twenties, danced around the floor in a special jogging rhythm, bodies not touching but dancing close and in pairs Most of the girls wore native dresses and turbans of bright cotton and their escorts looked hot but well-groomed in striped wool suits, shirts and neckties. Between dances, the couples sipped bottled beer or soft drinks and the whole garden had a genteel, country club atmosphere. Many British couples had come to dance (Nigeria has a population of over 33,000,000 with only 11,750 Europeans in residence), sitting alone or with Nigerian friends.

Later, we found a dance in a poorer section of Lagos where the crowd was much different—noisier, more raucous and younger. Two or three hundred of us were jammed into a big, mud-floored shed, so crowded that the trombone player barely had room to slide his instrument. Teen-agers and older dancers had come in couples, or just with groups of friends, some to dance, others to watch and beat time to the music. A few rickety tables leaned against the walls and here several girls sat, holding infants, wide-awake to the loud music, while younger children snuggled against them or fell asleep with heads on the tables. These baby-sitters and young mothers, passing their babies to the nearest stander-by to hold, were asked to dance just as frequently as girls who stood alone.

Most of the girls were miniatures of their older sisters, in loose cotton dresses and tied turbans, but the boys came in whatever they chose—shorts, loose shirts, long pants, cotton sweaters, bare feet—anything. One very young girl made her way in and out of the dancers selling refreshments, a fat, sleeping baby bound to her back and a flat wicker basket of hard-boiled eggs and little boxes of candied gum balanced carefully on her head. She did a brisk business and the baby slept soundly. These young dancers were not shy with strangers and I was asked to dance several times, with great courtesy, though I found the music a little too hot to follow. There is no color bar in Nigeria and the mood was gay, friendly and very informal.

Though he has no special girl and rarely even talks to girls, Idowu expects to get married at about twenty-five. "That is a good age for educated men to marry," he said confidently. "Here in Lagos, if an educated girl gets married before twenty or twenty-two, or a man before twenty-three or twenty-five, we think he doesn't want to make anything of himself. I will be married in the Church and I must marry a Christian."

In other parts of the country, marriage age and customs vary widely; many girls become brides in their teens, with parents demanding a "bride price" in the form of cattle or cash. In bush country, an attractive girl may bring as high as $150, while a more ordinary girl from an impoverished home may have a price of only about seventeen dollars. Nigerians favor chubby women and in many villages prospective brides are kept for several weeks in "the bride hut," where they are allowed no exercise and are fattened on feasts of yams before the ceremony.

One day, when the rain clouds hung above like a loose gray canopy, we drove through miles and miles of mangrove, forest and palm oil bush to the town of Ibadan, the largest Negro town in the world, with a dark-skinned population of half a million. On each side of the road, the forest rose like thick green walls, immense, silent and almost impenetrable, exuding an atmosphere of cool moisture. About once every ten miles, we passed a single roadworker, hacking at the growth along the roadside, fighting back the vegetation. Here and there were small bush villages, off narrow paths cut into the brush, simple clusters of straw-roofed huts that could not even be seen from a distance of ten feet away through the thick forest. Behind part of the forest wall lay palm oil plantations, with workers busy cutting the palm nuts for their valuable oil.

As yet, there is little organized industry in Nigeria and the country's chief exports are agricultural products—cocoa, palm kernels, palm oil and groundnuts (peanuts) and some cotton. The palm oil and the palm kernels (from which oil is pressed) are used over the world as a base for soap and other products. There are some large plantations but part of the supply is collected by free-lancers, chiefly women who gather the oil and sell it to small local dealers, who—in turn— sell it to bigger dealers in the larger cities. These small dealers are a frequent sight, whizzing along country trails on bicycles, with large oil cans attached on either side. Frequently, palm oil collected in the back country is stored in barrels. These barrels are then lashed together as a raft and floated down river to collecting centers. The palm oil tree has another use; its sap is collected and allowed to ferment for a few days to make a very intoxicating drink.

On the route to Ibadan we frequently passed "mammie wagons," the local buses going from village to village, ancient, wheezing and rocking on their axles. These vehicles are called "mammie wagons" because they so frequently carry the female market traders, burdened with goods. A few large villages sat close to the roadside—raw clearings of straw and mud huts but buzzing with activity and trade, every house facing the road set up as a market stall. Fortunately, we passed no more than ten motor vehicles on the two-hour ride, for every driver went at breakneck speed, even through the little towns. (I was reminded of something I read in a Lagos newspaper, in the "letters from our readers" column, under the provocative headline *What's So Special About Ducks?* A writer asked why people were so concerned about hitting ducks with their cars or bicycles. "No one cares about chickens or animals—why the worry about ducks?" For the next several days, the column was flooded with ominous answers which suggested: "Let us not forget our old beliefs. He who kills a duck by violence will next kill a human being by violence." Luckily, we hit no ducks, but we missed a full dozen children by inches only.

Ibadan is a miracle of confusion, a few cement-block houses on the outskirts of town, with outsized, staring flowers sticking out of the dry earth and the center of town a sea of tin shacks and people. Homes and market place were almost indistinguishable, since nearly every home carried on a business of some kind, many flamboyantly named: "Ike's World Famous Barber Shop," "Ye Old Fighting Cock Tavern—and bicycle parts," "Hollywood Starlet Dressmakers," etc. Women scurried through the crowd, selling food, usually a type of puffy doughnut or fried fish, carried in a wire cage on the head to keep out flies. Several lepers, faces swollen, arms diseased stumps, sat at the curbsides begging, looking —on the whole—not too miserable. Since Ibadan is the shopping center for much of this section of Nigeria, several full streets were devoted to fabric shops. Brilliant cotton cloth was stacked on the sidewalks like bales of hay and bright banners of color floated in the breeze from every doorway. The area itself was brown and dusty, shrill with voices and sprinkled with the confetti-coloring of bright fabric.

Off a side street, the "Paradise Club—for members only" seemed clean and cool, and we were welcomed cordially. Over a bottle of local beer, we sat listening to the hum of the city—and the conversation nearby. At the next table, two brightly-garbed Nigerians were chatting quietly. One said to his friend, "It doesn't pay for *me* to buy a good fountain pen—I just lose it." It was a problem so amusingly universal, so remote from heavy forests and dusty plains, that we might have been sitting in Milwaukee, Wisconsin.

Another day, we flew up to the prize city of the northern

region, Kano, a walled Moslem town with records to show it existed before Christ. Cities have color tones and Kano is a deep beige, tipped with white and overshadowed with a delicate, pale green from the graceful dome of the mosque that dominates the thick mud walls of the town itself. Most of the homes are made of "stabilized mud," a sturdy, sun-dried mixture that gives the place a squared-off look, though many of the walls are deeply grooved with long, featherlike designs, pressed into the mud. Frequently the individual house walls were peaked with small conelike parapets, white-washed with chalk. Even though many of the walls were eight to eleven feet tall, the whole town had a hand-molded, mud-pie effect, as if patted into place by a giant child.

The industry of the town is chiefly leather goods, soap— and peanuts. Several huge open fields outside the walls looked like circus encampments, but the great green tents were simply canvas covers protecting huge pyramids of bagged peanuts against the weather. Angular white cows grazed on the lawn of the city hall and colorful guards in bright red and green cotton uniforms stood before the houses of the local officials, adding color to the heart of town.

The sun was hot and every shadowed doorway appeared tempting as we wandered through the crooked streets; each house seemed to have a dozen people lounging in the cool dark just inside the door. An acrid stench led us to the dye merchants' neighborhood, where deep, stagnant pots of indigo, set into the earth, were used for dying lengths of cotton. (Indigo always has a sour smell and the big clay pots bubbled in the sun like stew left too long at the back of the stove.) Coupled with the cool white garb of the Moslems, deep indigo cotton is a favorite in the north and it is given a curious treatment to make it smooth and shiny, as if starched: around the dye pits were a series of little huts from which came the sounds of singing and pounding. Inside of each, five or six men crouched about a long log on which was stretched yards of wet, indigo-dyed cloth, and they chanted rhythmically as they beat at the cloth with wooden blocks. In the dusk of the huts, with faces and hands blue-blackened with dye, hands rising and falling over the cloth in unison, the men seemed mysterious and ritualistic, as if they were beating some living thing to death. Outside, in the bright sunlight, a rickety set of swings had been erected and children played and squabbled as if they were in Central Park. Little girls in Kano, from about six years on—until they withdraw in Moslem tradition—paint their faces in fantastic fashion, blue face powder, red lip coloring and dusky lines around the eyes. This, plus gay headcloths and dangling jewelry, makes them look like exaggerated gypsies, very pretty and very wild. Sheep wandered the street with the confidence of full-fledged citizens. On one occasion I entered a dim house to discuss buying a lion skin and was suddenly nudged deeper into the room from behind. It was not over-enthusiasm on the part of the seller—just four big, dusty sheep which had followed me through the doorway. Vultures, nature's garbage collectors, dotted the landscape, and one big bird sat peering through the hotel window as we ate lunch, eyes beady, head set low in a crust of dirty feathers.

In Kano, more than in any other cities, children, and even grown-ups, followed us everywhere, begging for *dash*. *Dash* is the local word for "tip" and a tip was wanted for everything. A group of workers shouted good-naturedly for *dash* when we stopped to watch them load peanuts on a freight car; children hoped for *dash* just for smiling as we passed them. In part, *dash* is based on the old tribal customs of offering gifts to the local chiefs and vice versa, but it also, unfortunately, extends through all phases of Nigerian life, from political appointments to securing scholarships. Then *dash* is synonymous with "graft," and is one of the real dangers to a potentially honest self-government.

A curious peace pervaded Kano—the clear skies, the symmetry of the architecture, the ever-present religious feeling symbolized by the huge mosque and the simplicity of the life. It is just an isolated town of stabilized mud, but with beauty of its own. A Lagos newspaperman who had seen London, Lisbon and New York said with conviction, "Once one has seen Kano, one never forgets."

Back in Lagos, Idowu Somnyiwa vowed that some day he, too, would go to Kano. He didn't know exactly where it was nor how far away but he felt "an educated man can go anywhere. I study every day." Thirty-three million Idowus, determined and working together, can re-shape their own world. As I left him, Idowu did not seem so small, after all.

12

POULETTE MAQUINAY

Belgium

LITTLE POULETTE MAQUINAY lives in Fraipont, a tiny village
of about two hundred people, a few snug cafes and a
steepled brick church, set in a lush Belgian valley, several
miles outside the city of Liege. Wide stretches of railroad
track straddle the village and the high wooded hills on either
side are often blued with train smoke. It is a disconnected

suburb, still rural and remote, to the ancient, sprawling, industrial city of Liege.

During World War II, over 20,000 buzz bombs landed in the Liege area, aimed to cripple industry and transportation, and many fell, too, in the quiet Fraipont valley. Villagers shared meager food and fuel with the American G.I.'s and the wooded hilltops hid scores of American gun crews with antiaircraft artillery trained on bomber planes and buzz-bomb aircraft that flew in from Germany, just a few miles away. Now the hilltops have grown over their scars and Fraipont is again a peaceful, prosperous village, living in the glamorous shadow of big sister, Liege.

Poulette is sixteen years old, tiny, shy and very pretty. She knows every man, woman, child and friendly dog that walks the Fraipont streets. The river, the hills, the red brick houses are as familiar as a well-worn picture hung before her eyes since she was born. Up one street is the public grade school, with fenced gravel yard and worn desks, where she studied till she was twelve; down another is the cafe, windows shining, flower boxes trim, where, with her mother and father, she sometimes shares a glass of Belgian beer; across town is the Catholic church where she made her First Holy Communion, hears Mass early every Sunday morning and will probably be married. Belgium is ninety per cent Catholic and Poulette is a devout teen-ager.

"My mother and father were born in Fraipont, too," she explains. "In fact, we were all born here—my older brother, my younger sister and I. Now I am in my last year at the professional school, run by the nuns. We have twenty-five students—all girls. Four are in my class. Our school is an old chateau and we each pay fifteen dollars a year to study there.

"Right now, my studies are in coutourie and shorthand. I have learned to sew and make patterns. I also study drawing for fashion and the stenographic shorthand. I made the skirt I have on and the sweater," she said proudly. Her skirt was a dark green corduroy, gored to flair out, and the sweater was knitted in coarse gray wool, long sleeved and V-necked, with an ingenious detachable turtleneck and inset, which could be removed in warmer weather. Poulette is very short, with fresh, fine skin and silky-clean hair. There was a village-shyness in her manner, but with a touch of perky chic that suggested poise and confidence underneath. Her hands were scrubbed and hard-worked but she wore pale pink lipstick and her hair was clipped gamin fashion.

"We Belgians are very busy people," she said, "and I am always busy, too. School starts at eight-forty-five each day and at noon I hurry home to help with the lunch. My grandmother lives with us and there are just the three of us—for the midday meal—my little sister, grandmother and me. My mother is a public nurse and is usually busy around the village. (In this country, it is not unusual for homemakers to combine home and career and about thirteen per cent of the women work.)

"At school, we study till four o'clock. Then I have time for games at school or just come home to help with the housework. I do not have time for much else except to listen to the radio or go to the cinema with my parents once in a while."

We sat in the parlor of Poulette's home as we talked, a small room with flowered wallpaper and big, plush-covered furniture. The day was so cold that our breath hung in the air. In the next room, her family lingered around the dining table, drinking after-dinner coffee and nibbling a big plate of rich pastries and cracked nuts after a full Sunday dinner. In that room, a fat coal stove blazed. The Maquinay house is typical of the village, a low, six-room, red brick structure, flush to the sidewalk, trim but old. Outside a hard snow was packed onto the ground and the wind from the hills whistled through the valley.

Belgium is a cozy country, plump, prosperous and progressive. It is a nation where new cars crowd the highways, smoke curls from kitchen chimneys and rows of hefty turkeys, necks festooned with dark feathers, hang in the butchers' windows, along with fat hams and bright wheels of cheese from nearby Holland. A tiny country, about the size of the state of Maryland, and with not many more people than there are in New York City, Belgium has survived German occupation and looting in two World Wars. It is land-lucky, with good farming, coal for mining and plenty of well-paid jobs for skilled workers. The country is crowded and the fields are small, but the rich countryside, dotted here and there with gawky windmills, boasts comfortable farms, with sturdy brick houses and well-tended fences.

It was St. Nicholas' Day and a Sunday, early in December, when I visited the Maquinays. In the cold parlor, a St. Nicholas Day table had been set out for the younger sister, saucers of hard candies and peanuts, a couple of big chocolate "wooden shoes" and giant gingerbreads, a foot tall, made of the hard, gummy native gingerbread, in shapes ranging from St. Nicks to sailboats and big, sugar-dotted figures of the Christ Child. Dolls, books and games were piled under the table, gifts from St. Nicholas, and burned-down red candles stood on the windowsills. The little sister had discovered the St. Nicholas treats, according to custom, when she got up in the morning—and the table would stand, decorations diminishing day by day, all through the Christmas season.

"When I finish school at the chateau, I hope to go into Liege, to study to be a medical secretary. I can take the train in each day and still live at home." (Liege is one of the five largest cities in Belgium and has many good schools, as well as excellent libraries and museums.)

Poulette, a village girl living so close to a big town, is self-conscious about what she terms her "too quiet life" and she stressed again and again that her mother and father were quite strict with her. "When my nineteen-year-old brother was at home, I sometimes was allowed out in the evening with him," she explained. "But he is away in the army now." (Belgium has an army of 142,000 well-trained men, equipped with modern weapons and each Belgian youth must spend eighteen months in military training.)

"Now I go to the movies when my parents go—and sometimes we all go walking in the evening. And I read a lot—mostly historical books and things about animals. And there is always the radio. We love jazz here and sometimes I listen to classical music."

Belgium is a home-loving country and Poulette's stay-at-home life is probably more typical than she thinks. Everywhere one gets the impression that the houses are comfortable—and that the families are inside them. Except for such ancient cities as Brussels and Bruge, much of the architecture of Belgium seems routine and unimaginative. "But," explained a Liegois, with a laugh, "much of our building was destroyed in the wars—both times we rebuilt quickly. Perhaps not beautifully but quickly!" In the villages and immediate suburbs, the red brick or yellow stucco houses stand row on row, commonly with lace curtains stretched tightly across the windows, then bowed in the middle into a kind of nipped waist with pastel ribbons. And in the evening, there is usually a car before each house.

Liege, even after heavy war damage, is a beautiful and busy city. The river Meuse winds through its parks, business and living area. In the center of town, many apartment buildings rise in modern gray stone, with wide, clear windows and neat, squared-off balconies. Block after block of new building has grown out of the war rubble till the city does not have a broken fence or cracked wall in sight. In Aachen, Germany—about an hour's car ride away—where some of the hardest fighting of the war took place, about one-third of the city still lies in grass-grown, caved-in ruin.

As the langorous, twisting Meuse winds out of the city of Liege, its banks are often crowded close with work-scuffed barges and dark, drab warehouses, grayed with train smoke; just outside the town, heaps of refuse from the coal mines have piled up until they are gentle mountains against the sky. But the people of Belgium do not mind the crowded, overly-industrial look that marks their big cities; such activity has given them economic security and the highest living standard of any country in Europe.

Liege is both homey and sophisticated. The city streets are bright at night with the neon lights of movie theaters, ballet performances draw crowds, restaurants are always filled with families out for a treat and the department stores are well supplied with modern furniture, cosmetic counters and television sets for sale. As an "old Europe" touch, flower stalls and stands for choice fruit and vegetables line the center of many boulevards.

City teen-agers here date much as they do in the United States, from about seventeen years old on. School is compulsory until fourteen years of age and those who go to higher school are usually serious students, but not too serious to indulge in a fad or two. College men sport a curious hat made of soft, dark suede, like a big beret but with a short visor over the eyes, bristling with pins and trophies—school and club pins—sports emblems and plastic shapes of girls' heads, flowers and good luck charms. Belgian girls dress much like American teen-agers, except perhaps a little warmer, with sheepskin lined shoes for school in winter, a couple of sweaters under a suit coat and a big wool kerchief to tie over the ears.

Belgians love good food and they are lucky enough to have a lot of it. Typical of the appetite of the country is the food specialty known as *fries* and advertised that way on every little cafe in the country. We stopped for some *fries* on a night so cold that the windows of the cafe were steamed opaque. A huge iron stove glowed in one corner, the television set was on full blast, tuned to a variety show from Paris, and at several tables comfortably dressed men sat playing dominoes and sipping beer. The cafe was redolent of coal heat and comfort. The *fries,* cooked and served by the proprietor's wife, was a big piece of steak, cut thin and fried crisp, and a huge tureen of French fried potatoes, still sizzling from the hot fat. This was immaculately served with homemade tomato relish, glasses of ice water and paper napkins, the latter a luxury in Europe. At other taverns, the *fries* might be small river trout, instead of meat, but always with a generous portion of fried potatoes. The coffee shop-bakery is also a popular Belgian hangout—a bakery with a few neat tables in the back, at which customers may stop for coffee and a choice of the pastries fresh from the oven. Often, on a cold day, to walk off the street into one of these snug shops, warm, sweet and spicy, with trays of cakes, tarts and fresh bread on display is as sense-stimulating as stepping into a tropical greenhouse full of exotic blooms.

In this prosperous country, few students hold part-time jobs "except," explained Poulette, "to help our mothers around the house. I take over our house in the summertime, all but the two weeks when I go on vacation. Each summer, through the church youth group, some girl friends and I go to live on a farm. And once, with a school group, we took a two-day bus trip into Holland."

Every month, Poulette's father gives her a twenty-dollar allowance (he is employed as an industrial draftsman at a factory outside Liege), out of which she is expected to buy her clothes (usually she buys material, makes the clothes herself in school) and take care of school expenses. Some day she hopes to save up enough money to take a long trip, probably to Spain. Why to Spain? "Well," said Poulette, "I hear the country is beautiful and the people are kind. And besides, I have never seen a poor country."

Most of Poulette's ideas about the United States have come from movies and from magazines. "I think of your country as a land of skyscrapers, with no farmers," she said with a teasing smile. "Your life is a life of businessmen and everyone has lots of riches. But," she added defensively, "money doesn't make happiness. I believe, too, that your young people have a life different from ours. They are more free and go out every night."

Though many G. I.'s crowded into her village during the war, Poulette remembers almost nothing about them. Except for the fear of bombs, only one special incident from the war stuck in her childish mind: a group of German soldiers swarmed into her father's shop one day (he ran a bicycle shop at the time) and demanded that he repair their bikes. When the job was finished, the Germans refused to pay. Poulette's single memory is lighthearted and harmless compared to the anti-German stories most villagers have to tell. Two wars, great suffering and loss of life in this brave little country have made most Belgians permanently bitter against their German neighbors. Though both countries now work and trade as friends, it is impossible to consider Belgian life without remembering how it has been affected by wars.

And Belgium is a "different" nation for still another reason: a part of her distinctive prosperity comes from a distant, dark-skinned child, the Belgian Congo. Belgium is the mother country to this vast area in the middle of Africa, a territory eighty times her own size. The Congo has belonged to Belgium since 1878, when it was simply "grabbed" by the famous journalist-explorer, Henry Morton Stanley, in the name of the greedy and enterprising King Leopold II. "Dividing Africa" was popular sport for powerful European nations in those days, and for about thirty years this territory of 902,000 square miles, one-third the size of the United States, and all its revenues were the personal property of Leopold II. The early days of this control were marked by unbelievable cruelty and unfairness to the Congolese and the population shrank from 20,000,000 to the 12,000,000 natives there are today. Finally, at the insistence of other nations outraged at the atrocities, Leopold was forced to sign over all rights and controls of the Belgian Congo to the Belgian government.

Today, the Belgians run the territory with kindness and imagination and plan eventually to turn the entire area back to the Congolese for self-rule. The Congo is one of the richest lands on earth and, among its many products, it has provided fifty per cent of the world's uranium supply. As a dutiful child, it turns over most of its earnings to the mother country, thus helping to keep Belgium the snug, fat country it is.

Teen-aged Poulette summed up the admirable and interesting Belgian personality, herself included, when she said, "We are just a little country surrounded by other countries, but we are *different*. We laugh more than the *Dutch* but we are less gay and chic than the *French;* we are more honest and warmhearted than the *Germans*—and we work harder than anybody on *earth!*"

13

FOOD, FUN AND CUSTOMS

Morocco

TANGIER, though on the north coast of Africa, is a city of "many countries." It is now a part of the Sultanate of Morocco, but for many years Tangier was an international city, governed by a board of several countries. It is a gleaming, new, white "skyscraper" town, rapidly growing up around the old, crumbling walled city of the Arabs, the casbah. Though the food of many nations is served here, the most popular cooking is Arab, English, Spanish or French. In fact, so mixed is the national character of the city that even the street signs are printed in three languages.

The best Arab food in the city is served in the casbah and bought at the giant street market, which is open every Thursday and Sunday. (In the Moslem religion, Friday is observed as the Holy Day and not only the market but most shops are closed that day.) The food market is a crowded area of open-air stalls that covers several city blocks. Produce is divided by type, with fruit stalls lined together, vegetables at their feet or a few tiny chickens, still alive, with feet bound, eyes staring beadily at the crowd. In the summertime, the market is a-buzz, not only with flies, but with hundreds and hundreds of minute honeybees that hover over the open trays of colored candies, heaps of grapes and the great mounds of fresh dates. At noon, when the sun is high, the merchants go from table to table, splashing pails of cold water over the garden things, to keep them from drying out in the sun. Since the strictly religious Arabs refuse to drink anything alcoholic, hot mint tea is the favorite drink and the mint stalls cover a whole block, the tables piled high with bunches of fresh, extra-large mint that fills the air with a crisp fragrance. The bustle, the colorful clothes of the Arabs and the thin, weird music played by street musicians give the market place the air of an oriental carnival.

Mint tea is the favorite drink in the sidewalk cafes and at home. Since it is against the tradition for Arab women to sit in cafes or public restaurants, the little tables are crowded with men only, talking, doing business—and sipping at glasses of mint tea. This drink is made of green tea, served very hot in little glasses, highly sweetened and poured over several sprigs of fresh mint crowded into the glass. To keep from

[207]

burning the fingers, the glass is always held with the thumb on the upper rim and the first finger firmly under the thick glass bottom. The tea is fragrant and refreshing and the Arabs, even when wrapped in their thick wool *djellabas*, always look cooler than those foreigners, lightly dressed, who insist on drinking gin and tonic or cold beer.

Cous cous, an Arab specialty of hot buttered wheat germ, served with chicken and other vegetables, is usually the basis of any Arab feast. (A true feast is called a *diffa* and at the home of wealthy Moroccans, such a feast may have as many as thirty different courses. There is a theory of hospitality behind such lavishness: the guest is meant to feel welcomed by the extreme generosity of his host. But even at a *diffa,* nothing is wasted. The dishes are tasted and nibbled at the table by the host and his male guests. Then each dish is served to the women of the household, dining in another room. What is left is then welcomed as dinner for the servants.)

A typically excellent Moroccan menu is the following, served at *A Thousand and One Nights,* a candle-lit Arab restaurant in the casbah of Tangier.

First, a very hot vegetable soup, with bits of tomato and green pepper, flavored lightly with cinnamon and topped with a thin slice of lemon.

Then an omelette, very thin, made with finely chopped fresh parsley and garlic and tiny pink shrimp, all sprinkled sparingly with sugar just before serving.

Cous cous served in individual bowls, heaped steaming over cooked chicken. The *cous cous* is garnished with strips of cooked carrots, a circle of chick peas and almonds and very fat, sweet raisins. This is accompanied by hot and sweet sauces, and guests use small napkins of colored toweling while eating, since the chicken is picked up with the fingers. In true Arab fashion, the *cous cous* should be handled with the fingers, too, formed first into mouth-sized bits and popped into the mouth like ping-pong balls.

The fourth course was pigeon pie, an exquisite delicacy, only about half an inch thick, with fine, flaky crust and a filling of minced pigeon meat and spice, served very hot.

The dessert was thin slices of oranges, chilled and served with a spoonful of "sauce," simply sugar-water in which jasmine blossoms had been soaked until they left their exotic fragrance. Last came mint tea, poured from a small, ornate silver pitcher.

In some Arab restaurants, there is a floor show, an exhibition of dancing by young boys in their early teens. Since it would be against Moslem tradition to have respectable women or girls dance in public (though wealthy Moroccans sometimes keep groups of private dancers), the boys go through intricate steps and girations that suggest female dancers. (In the days of Shakespeare, too, it was against tradition for women to appear on the stage, and all female parts were played by young boys.)

Thirst is always a problem in this country with its hot African sun and miles of near desolate road through arid plains and rugged mountains. Occasionally, whole villages or a group of nearby farms are supplied by a single well, with a dusty camel plodding round and round in a still dustier circle, drawing water. Along well-traveled roads, one comes frequently on small tin and shingle shacks, huddled by the roadside, with a pile of soft drinks and a dozing Arab waiting for thirsty travelers. Carbonated orange is the favorite drink, taken un-iced and straight from the bottle.

In the heat of a Moroccan summer day, melons are a valued food and "drink." A bit of shade and a heap of melons always bring a tired customer, eager to rinse the dust from his mouth. Many of the little melons, like small cantaloupes, are no larger than baseballs, but deliciously sweet and juicy.

One sweltering afternoon in late August, I sat in on the equivalent of an Arab musical jam session. With Ahmed Mohammed Boonan, a young Moroccan friend of mine, I walked through the angled streets of the old casbah in Tetuan, into the "square of the tailors," where the Berber women in their coarse country garments and cartwheel straw hats sat on the cool cobblestones, hawking baskets and strips of hand-woven cloth and gabbling like turkeys. In the dark open-fronted shops around the small square, master tailors fashioned garments, taking fine, expert stitches or working cross-legged on small sewing machines that whirred noisily in the hot afternoon. Around them hopped tailors' apprentices, little boys of eight to eleven, pulling basting threads, pressing, holding spools or running errands for the master.

At one corner of the square, we turned up a narrow stone staircase, the first step a full two feet up from the ground. On the third floor of the old building was a long, narrow room, hazy with smoke and humming with a strange, high music. We ordered bottled orange at one of the rickety wood tables. Around us sat a dozen or so men, each with his bottled orange or mint tea. They were puffing contentedly on small hashish pipes with carved wooden stems about ten inches long and tiny clay bowls no bigger than a thimble. At the far end of the room were the musicians, squatting on straw mats around a low table set with bowls of great roses and yellow iris. There were five musicians in all, playing a violin, a little blue and yellow plastic flute, two giant steel-stringed guitars and a tambourine, plus a drum made of pottery with a skin top. The drum and tambourine were both manipulated by the same man, as he leaned lethargically against the cool stone wall.

The musicians played on and on, from one number to another, in a high singsong cadence, one or the other stopping now and then to sip tea or puff at a common hashish pipe resting on the table. The men in the cafe chanted along in soft, high voices, beating the tables lightly with their finger tips. A few dozed in their chairs. The strange rhythm, the hashish smoke and the heat of the day gave the afternoon a hypnotic, drowsy quality. It was like listening to a gathering of huge human insects, giving out a strange, droning musical hum.

Much of the time I was in Morocco, the atmosphere was very tense. Many Moroccans were still bitter against their former "protectors," the French, and there were raids, bombings and killings throughout the country. We were warned to "keep off back country roads" and therefore I did not see as much of the remote mountain life as I might have in more peaceful times. However, because it gives such a good picture of human life, and mountain pleasure, I asked top reporter Barrett McGurn of the *New York Herald*

Tribune if I might use his account of a celebration given by Berber mountain tribesmen for French Lt. General Pierre Boyer de Latour, near the town of El Mer, in the Atlas Mountains. Mr. McGurn was also a guest at the feast and described it this way:

"The feast was a typical Berber mountain party. Four thousand tribesmen, most of them shepherds or peasant farmers, gathered their women folk for dancing, singing and eating.

"The women were tattooed mountain fashion. Crosses and zigzag lines curved over their cheeks and chins like men's sideburns and goatees.

"Other tattoo marks were on the tips of noses, on the lips, in the middle of the forehead, round the fingers like rings and around the ankles like socks. Some of the women had the palms of their hands and the backs of their fingers stained red.

"The food was also typical of the annual feasts. The first course was a fried flat bread stuffed with chicken and eggs and covered with powdered sugar.

"The next course was roast sheep served whole and torn apart and eaten with three fingers of the right hand.

"The third course was turkey served with almonds. The fourth course was a platter of three chickens for every six guests. The chickens were covered with olives.

"The fifth course was *cous cous,* a wheat paste in grains smaller than BB shots, served in tiny bowls. Bananas, grapes and pears washed down with mint tea finished the feast and finished off a good number of the guests as well. A large part of the general's party dozed in their automobiles as they started the trip back.

"As the general and his guests ate, the men and women of the tribe did the local dance. They stood hip-to-hip in a long line jiggling up and down and undulating back and forth while they sang in high-pitched voices both flattering and ironic impromptu songs about the career of General Boyer de Latour. The general started his career as a young officer near here."

Spain

For most Spaniards, breakfast is eaten between eight and nine in the morning and it nearly always consists of the same thing: thick bread or toast, with butter and marmalade, and strong black coffee, mixed half and half in an outsized cup with boiling milk and sugar. A favorite *early* morning breakfast of many hard working Spaniards is *café con leche* (coffee with milk) and chunks of bread dipped in saucers of pure olive oil.

The hours set for lunch and dinner are "halfway between," by American standards. Lunch is served around one-thirty for the working folk and around three for wealthier Spaniards, at home or at smart restaurants. Dinner in the evening comes at nine o'clock, if you're one of the people who have to be up early in the morning; otherwise ten or eleven is a fashionable hour to sit down to dinner. We went to a dinner dance in Valencia and our first course—a fish soup—was set on the table at the stroke of midnight. Of course, a wandering gypsy or a poor workman is glad to eat his chunk of bread and stalk of sugar cane at any hour, but for most Spaniards, mealtimes are a serious business.

[213]

Luncheon is commonly four courses and dinner, considered a light repast, rarely less than three. Spaniards like grace and color with their meals and frequently a carafe (a globe-shaped bottle with a narrow neck) of red or white wine is served with a twist of fresh green leaves as a stopper and a large basket of dessert fruit may be decorated with green leaves or an arrangement of deep purple bougainvillea blossoms.

In Spain, most stores and businesses are closed each day from one o'clock till four. Businessmen take siestas at home after lunch and many workmen just curl up on the job, coats over their heads, for a brief nap. Around six o'clock, when the afternoon has cooled off and there are still at least three hours to go till dinner time, many women take time out for their *merienda* of tea or chocolate with cakes and pastries— usually very fancy pieces of pastry art, filled with jams and dusted with powdered sugar. This is probably the most "fattening" time of the day in Spain. For men, a glass of wine and *tapis* in a cafe breaks up the long stretch until dinner time. Tapis means any tasty bit of food, such as we might call an appetizer: a plate of tiny, in-the-shell clams cooked with vinegar and spices, sliced sausage, a tiny roast bird, a sliver of fried steak on bread or simply salted nuts and olives.

Here are some typical Spanish foods, all popular with Spaniards. Certain of these have become favorites in parts of the United States, too.

Entremeses variados—commonly a first course to luncheon —is a variety of as many as fourteen different appetizing dishes, all served on separate plates and in tiny portions.

The *entremeses* might include sliced tomatoes, salted almonds, sardines, olives, sliced garlic sausage, tuna fish, goat cheese, boiled chick peas, cold artichoke, sliced pimiento, fried squid, cold boiled shrimp in the shell, hard-boiled egg with mayonnaise and thin ham. This ham is called *jamon serrano* or mountain ham. It is not smoked for curing but is laid out in the sun, on the snow of the mountains. The snow preserves while the sun cures. It is dark red when served and sliced so thin that the pieces look translucent. It is also quite expensive and even a small slice is considered a treat.

Paella might almost be called Spain's national dish, since it is popular and well-cooked in every part of Spain. The best *paella* is reputed to be made in Valencia, in the rice growing area on the east coast of Spain. *Paella* is a dish with a rice foundation, mixed with saffron, which gives it a bright yellow color. To it are added bits of seafood—tiny shrimp, clams in their shells, flakes of fish, bits and circles of *calamares* (squid or octopus) and pieces of fried chicken, beef, with green peas, all topped off with strips of red pimiento. *Paella* is cooked on top of the stove, in a big *paella* pan, usually copper but sometimes made of pottery, in country kitchens. When the rice is fluffy, every grain separate, the *paella* is ready. It is always served right in the pan in which it is cooked. Such pans are only about two to three inches deep but a big family or restaurant-size container may measure a foot and a half across.

Gazpacho is a summer soup that has social-climbed out of the poor peasant kitchen into the best restaurants in Madrid.

It is an iced soup (in the bigger towns where ice is available) made with a base of oil and vinegar, to which is added strained tomatoes, garlic, bread crumbs, finely chopped cucumbers, green pepper and a little onions. Croutons of garlic toast are sometimes put in at the last moment. Spaniards find it refreshing, either after a long day with a donkey cart or after a social afternoon, looking over the Goya and Velasquez masterpieces at the Prado Museum.

It's a cheerful day in Spain when the little restaurants and bars can print on their windowpanes with whitewash: *"Hay angulas!!!"* (*"Angulas* today!!!"*) That means the fish catch was good and the cook can serve up a dish of these tiny, silvery eels, probably several hundred to a portion, since each is about an inch long and not much wider than a rubber band. They are cooked in small pottery dishes, sizzling in hot olive oil, with garlic and slivers of red-hot peppers. *Angulas* are always eaten with a wooden fork and most Spaniards eat everything in the dish except the last bits of hot pepper. One windy winter day, we sat in a small seaside cafe in the old port town of Cadiz. It was a Sunday afternoon, the day of a big football match between the Cadiz team and nearby Algeciras. Men jammed the tables and the bar, eating sizzling *angulas* and drinking cold white wine, while the radio blared the game in the background. Had the game been baseball and the *angulas* and wine just pretzels and beer, the scene would have been typically American.

Postres, which is the Spanish word for "dessert," can mean many things, but it usually means a big basketful of local fruit, including apples, peaches, apricots, oranges (often picked in the back garden), grapes and cherries. Fruit is so

[216]

popular in Spain that a hearty eater might easily consume
three or four pieces as dessert, all rinsed carefully in the
bowls of water set on the table with the fruit.

In spite of the fact that Spain is a land of orange orchards,
orange juice is rarely served in the home. However, Spanish
housewives have devised a delicately fresh dessert with a juice
base: fresh-hulled strawberries served chilled, with a small
pitcher of orange juice to pour over instead of cream.

Goat's cheese, a fine-grained white cheese with a definite
"goat taste" to it, is served sliced thin after many meals. The
little goat, traveling in herds along the highways and butting
and jostling over the thin grass of the mountains, thrives in
Spain and the people consider goat's cheese a healthful
delicacy.

Carne de membrillo, as popular with Spanish children as
jello is with most young Americans, is sometimes passed off
to grown-ups, too, as "dessert." It's a sweet, jelly-like sub-
stance that is sold in cellophane-wrapped rectangles, then cut
thin for serving. Quince fruit, gelatin and a few other odds
and ends go into *carne de membrillo* and it tastes like apple
sauce, over-sweetened and burned brown. A country restaurant, filling out its menu with a show of elegance, may
well serve fruit, goat's cheese and *carne de membrillo* as the
dessert course.

Jugo de frutos is a cool drink very popular with big-city
teens as an after-movie (but in the afternoon, of course)
refreshment. However, it costs about fifteen cents a glass
and therefore must be considered a rare treat by most. It is

[217]

a combination of fruits (the name means simply "juice of fruits"), whipped into a creamy pulp in an electric mixer, much like a malted milk. The base is orange juice, to which may be added a few slices of apple, a banana, some straw-berries, half a peach, etc. It is served in a tall glass with straws—and a chance at seconds out of the mixer for those who drink up fast!

"*Caramelos, caramelos*" is a familiar cry up and down the streets of Spain. When a young boy or wrinkled grandmother in black wants to earn some money, he or she sets up busi-ness on the doorstep or along the streets with a tray of *caramelos*. The word itself means "caramel" but it is used to describe almost any kind of simple candy or sweet, usually a fruit drop wrapped in colored paper. These trays of candy see all weather, baking in the sun outside the bull ring on scorching summer afternoons or dampening with mist in the cold months of winter. So very often, the *caramelos* are stale treats. The more prosperous *caramelos* vendors set up tiny moveable stands in the parks or along the village streets during fiesta time, adding such things as peanuts in the shell, cooked and sweetened chick peas served in a twist of brown paper, and bubble gum. When a Spaniard takes his girl for a Sunday afternoon or early evening promenade, they some-times split a peseta's worth of *caramelos*. Two and a half cents (a peseta) buys two pieces of brightly wrapped candy, enough to add a fillip to a pleasant walk in the park.

Most of the food of Spain is cooked in olive oil, and, though the oil is heavy for foreign stomachs, the Spaniards love it. A favorite food for breakfast or late at night is a

[218]

churro—a kind of doughnut about as thick as a man's finger, with a three-inch diameter. *Churro* sellers set up business on busy sidewalks, with a vat of smoking olive oil placed over a charcoal flame and batter which is squeezed out of a tube into the fat. The crisp *churros* are fished from the fat, brown and sizzling, on a stick and two are strung together with a piece of grass to sell for a peseta. In the side streets of big towns such as Madrid and Barcelona, the midnight air and the first smells of morning are heavy with the hot, fatty odor of fresh *churros*.

France

Throughout the world, "French cooking" means "good cooking," and it is true that the French love food and cook it with a respect and understanding that makes it excellent, from the smallest cafe to famed Maxim's in Paris.

The French believe that good food is one of the pleasures of life and always take time to enjoy their meals. (To them, the American cafeteria or the "sandwich and malted" lunch is sheer madness.) Most places of business are closed from one to three, to give time for a good, leisurely lunch. The supermarket is almost unknown in France and, though there are many small food stores, much like our delicatessens, most of the food shopping is done in open-air markets, scattered everywhere through the main streets and living areas of the towns.

In Paris, for instance, the Rue de Seine, a narrow, crowded street of shops and homes, is converted each day from about seven o'clock in the morning until two in the afternoon into a busy, open-air market place. There are some shops with fronts open completely to the street. Other merchants set up pushcarts or temporary stalls with canvas roofs. During the market hours, the street bustles with shoppers, carrying baskets or string shopping bags (there is very little paper to wrap purchases and few packaged goods). By three in the afternoon, every stand is out of sight and the street is closed —until tomorrow.

Each merchant deals in one product only—fresh eggs come from one stall, meat from another, cheese from another, fresh vegetables from another, etc. Occasional stalls sell buttons, ribbons, dish cloths, baking dishes—anything a busy house-wife might need. The whole market place, like hundreds set up all over Paris every morning, has the rushed and colorful look of a fair grounds. The French love the artistic and picturesque, and every meat shop, with its heavy, butch-ered carcasses of veal or bony, skinned tails of beef hanging from hooks, also has a pot of violets or a bunch of fresh carnations sitting next to the cash register. Most housewives shop "by the day," purchasing fresh each morning all the food needed for that day alone (iceboxes are still a rarity), so going to market is also a social outlet, a place to meet and talk with friends. Many a chic homemaker goes through the market place in a neat, dark-colored dress, a touch of lipstick and smart pearl earrings, properly dressed for town.

Most of the food for the neighborhood markets is pur-chased in the early morning hours from a giant central market called Les Halles. Several city blocks square, this wholesale center is ringed in by huge trucks which have carried produce from all parts of France to arrive fresh at the city. Again, the French like to show their sense of the artistic, even in business, and carrots are piled higher than a man's head in bright patterns of orange with feathery green stems, while boxes of strawberries, heads of cabbage, crates of oranges are arranged to dazzle the eye and lure buyers. A special section of the market is filled with stalls of fresh flowers, and fragrance from the blooms, joined with the brilliance of the lights, the bright colors of the foods, gives Les Halles an exaggerated, dreamlike quality. Of course, this great market is a place of shrewd and serious business, designed to supply the third largest city in the world with fresh food each day.

On the rim of the market place are several early morning restaurants, crowded not only with market porters and market gardeners, but with Parisians out for a late night. About five o'clock one morning, we visited the restaurant, Le Chat Qui Fume (The Cat Who Smokes), ate hot onion soup, crusted with grated cheese, and danced to a tiny jazz band while the sun came up and streamed through the windows into the blue, smoky room.

Sidewalk cafes are popular through all the warm countries of Europe and especially so in France. When people live in small, simple apartments, the neighborhood cafes serve as an extra living room, a social club, a place to meet friends. When the first ray of spring sun shows in France, the cafe owner puts out as many little tables and chairs as can be crowded onto the square or strip of sidewalk in front of his cafe. Sitting there to watch passers-by is a favorite pastime, relaxing and cheap, since a man may sit all afternoon with his newspaper and one glass of wine or cup of coffee. Many students, attending universities or art schools where campus space and study rooms are scarce, go to neighborhood cafes between classes, filling the tables with their books.

The French are not only proud of themselves as cooks but also as connoisseurs of food. As an example of this, I remember lunching one day at Maxim's, one of the best restaurants in Paris and even one of the best in the world. It is an elegant, expensive restaurant where the cuisine is considered excellent and one may order anything desired— at a price as high as fifteen dollars a person or more. We were looking at the menu when an elderly Frenchman was ushered in, dignified and impressive, with well-groomed mustache and a carnation in his buttonhole. He examined the menu for a while and then laid it aside. The waiter wheeled over the hors d'ouevre cart and the gentleman studied the cold lobster, the chilled vegetables, the imported sardines—and then motioned the food aside. Next came the hot meat cart, and the waiter lifted back the giant polished hood, showing a ham, crusted with sweets, and a perfectly cooked roast of beef, sizzling over hidden burners. The gentleman was not pleased. He looked over the cheese tray with a selection of a dozen different cheeses and then glanced at the pastry cart, with its creamy cheese cakes, fresh strawberry tarts and a half dozen other pastries. Sadly he shook his head and ordered a glass of bottled water. He drank it slowly, then thanked the waiters and left. He was ushered out with the same ceremony and courtesy with which he had been shown in. The waiters respected his decision. As a Frenchman, he had the right to take his food seriously. The food at Maxim's that day did not pass *this* Frenchman's standards.

A French family usually spends a third of its income for food and the day begins with breakfast, around seven or eight in the morning—either a big cup of coffee and milk or a cup of strong chocolate, with freshly baked croissants, a kind of flaky breakfast roll, crisp on the outside and shaped like a half-moon. The housewife or a wide-awake child customarily dashes out to get the croissants fresh from the baker's for each breakfast. Except for hotels especially catering to tourists, it is impossible to find a different breakfast anywhere in France. Many working men like to stop on their way to work for a small cup of hot coffee, laced with a glass of rum, as an additional starter for the day.

Lunch is eaten between one and three and dinner after eight o'clock in the evening. Both meals are usually served in three courses, sometimes four. Unlike an American "plate lunch," with everything served at once, the Frenchman prefers to eat first something such as pickled herring with onions, sardines with lemon or a salad of finely sliced tomatoes in oil and vinegar. Then comes a meat course with salad, followed by dessert, usually cheese or fruit, and a cup of strong black coffee. Most adult Frenchmen (and even many children) drink wine with meals twice a day. Wine-making is one of the principal industries of France and table wine is very inexpensive. The wine is delivered to many big-city shops in tank trucks, such as we use for transporting gasoline and milk, and it is piped into vats in the cellar through trapdoors in the sidewalk. Most French housewives, coming from market, have a bottle of wine and a bunch of flowers sticking out of the market basket.

Bread is one of the most important and best-tasting items on a French menu and most families prefer to buy it fresh before each meal. A little schoolboy in a blue smock often stops to buy a loaf on his way home at noontime and, in the evening, one can see workmen riding home on bicycles with the long, brown, family-sized loaves balanced on the handle bars. The bread comes in three sizes (and is always sold unwrapped): *une flute*—the family-sized loaf, which is about eight inches around and nearly two feet long; the middle-size, which is called *une baquette;* and *une ficelle,* a loaf only about three inches around, crisp on the outside and extra fine inside. The French eat bread with everything, often laying a whole loaf on the table, allowing the family to cut off slices as they wish.

Escargots or snails are a French delicacy and they are served hot, still tight in their curved shells. First they are rinsed clean, then the shell is stuffed with a mixture of butter, salt, fine garlic and chopped fresh parsley. They are baked and served very hot, to be eaten with little long-pronged forks. Twelve of the little snails is considered a generous portion.

Soupe de chou or cabbage soup is popular throughout France and it is a very good big-family dish. All through the farm country, even when a light snow is on the ground, the gardens are filled with cabbage plants, usually a long, leafy cabbage that stands as high as a foot and a half out of the

[224]

ground. Served with local wine and chunks of crusty bread, it can make a full meal for a hard-working peasant—or a hungry tourist.

More than any single nation in the world, Frenchmen are fond of *camping*. When the first spring day turns warm, until the last chill of autumn, French highways are a-hum with vacationers, on loaded bicycles or in little French cars top-heavy with camping gear. Whole families take to the road. The exquisite South of France woods and beaches are favorite camping spots and in the height of the season the roads are nearly impassable around Juan-les-Pins and Nice because of the traffic of campers. Large wooded areas are set aside for camping, with small plots and cooking facilities rentable for a fee. Disgruntled hotel men and shop owners call the campers "our locusts" because they cover the land and live on so little.

However, French apply their characteristic chic to camping, too. They ride often on tandem-plus bicycles, with mother and father peddling hard, the little children balanced on seats behind. Sometimes the whole family is outfitted in matching shorts and shirts, making a pretty picture as they puff along the mountain roads. In camping equipment, tastes often run to bright stripes in tents, brilliant colors in camping chairs and even down as far as the decorous beaches of southern Spain, French women campers brighten the sands in their slim, colorful, two-piece swimming suits.

Portugal

The Portuguese claim to have a common saying (though I never heard anyone say it but a tourist guide): "Drink wine and one thousand Portuguese will have bread!!" The vineyards of Portugal are famous the world over and especially for the port wine which comes from areas around the Atlantic coast city of Porto, an industrial rival of Lisbon. The grapevines, originally imported from the fields of French Burgundy, thrive in rocky, arid ground, in an area where the beating sun keeps the air at hothouse temperature for months on end and the soil and sun hold the secret for the excellent wine-making qualities of the grape. Port wine is one of the major exports of this little country and there are several varieties, of course: a dry port for before meals, a fruity port for desserts and a more full-bodied port for more serious after-dinner drinking. (Port originally gained its reputation as the favorite wine of British monarchs.) I got my first taste of port wine on a bus tour through Lisbon. Our final stop was the Port Wine Institute, where each traveler was given a tiny dish of salted nuts and a big glass of port wine. It was a warm, rich wine, surprisingly strong and good—so good, in fact, that we were minus three passengers when the bus left for the center of town!

Fish is naturally one of the most important foods in this seacoast country. It is often routinely served and is simply "fried fish and boiled potatoes" at many meals. But a good housewife or a talented chef in an elegant restaurant can

[226]

make fish dishes memorable. Very often, peasant recipes are dressed up to become the featured items on expensive menus. Take *bacalhau* or codfish, for instance. This food is considered Portugal's national dish, but it tasted best, not in some seaside malet, but when it was given the prima donna treatment at one of Portugal's best restaurants, Tagide in Lisbon. The dining room of the restaurant opens onto a great balcony overlooking the picturesque Lisbon harbor and the lights are candlelight and the reflections of the lights from boats or the moon on the sea. The *bacalhau* was served in small, individual casseroles, in a bed of thinly sliced cooked onions, all covered with a cream sauce and grated cheese, heated till it bubbled. The Portuguese love *bacalhau* and at the Tagide they gave it everything but a roll of drums for its dramatic entrance.

Fado singers are a Portuguese phenomena and "Amalia," the leading female *fado* singer in the country, is as familiar in her homeland as Bing Crosby is in America. The *fado* is a poignant, sometimes harsh and wailing kind of song; traditionally the women singers wear black shawls around their shoulders and the song is accompanied by a guitar and viol. Many little restaurants, picturesque with checked tablecloths and rough stone floors, have *fado* singers as evening entertainment and the audience sips wine or beer and eats (at least at our table) a huge plate of clams, tiny and still in the shell, steamed in a mixture of water, a little olive oil, chopped red peppers and onions. These clams have the same "have more!" quality as peanuts in the shell and an extra plate is put on the table to hold the empties.

[227]

Fish is also a popular snack at every village bar—sardines in oil, cold shrimp served in the shell or large crayfish, cooked bright pink and chilled but still looking too much like specimens for a biology class, and large crabs, with just a sliver of meat in each claw. The Portuguese nibblers also love giant, yellowish chick peas, boiled in very salted water, then served cold. They slip easily out of a tough outer skin and taste a little like mealy peanuts. In simpler cafes, the shells of chick peas and fish are tossed to the floor and village cats poke and paw about, searching for overlooked tidbits.

Sweet desserts are highly popular in Portugal, especially delicate, rich pastries and cakes. No package of sweet rolls, sticky with simple frosting and all wrapped up in cellophane will do for the Portuguese connoisseur! Each cake and tart is a small work of art, decked and trimmed with cut cherries, twists of whipped cream and dashes of powdered sugar, either to be eaten at ease at a sidewalk cafe or carried home carefully in a box, right side up. Candied fruit is also a great delicacy and the town of Setubal is famous for its candied oranges. We bought some in a small wax cup, complete with little plastic spoon, and found it tasted like a hopped-up marmalade, so sugared and crystallized that it was almost "brilliantly" sweet.

After *fruit,* which is good and plentiful, *goat's cheese* probably ranks third as the nation's most popular dessert. The varieties range from coarse, porous cheese, so hard it takes a sharp knife to cut it, to very fine, smooth white cheese. But in taste it is always rather strong. Though it is

[228]

quite possible to eat most ordinary cheese without thinking of a cow, it is almost impossible to eat goat cheese without remembering the goat!

Germany

In Germany, there is a great emphasis on family life and fun at home. This—plus the fact that this country invariably has "white winters"—makes it a wonderful place to be at Christmastime.

We spent one December 25 in the picture-postcard loveliness of old Munich. For several weeks before, all of Germany had been getting ready for the great holiday season. In shops and big department stores, there was gay tinsel, ornaments and music much like in the United States; in every butcher shop, geese hung from the ceiling, fat and plucked clean, except for a ruff of feathers around the neck. Bakery shops were fragrant with special Christmas cakes and cookies and stores everywhere sold the traditional German Christmas candy: little pink pigs—from mother-size down to piglets about an inch long—made of sweet marzipan (a combination of sugar, ground almonds, etc.) with chocolate eyes and tails. Gingerbread, the hard, flat kind, is also a holiday favorite with German children, in decorated forms, from angels and dogs to candy-trimmed cottages.

Late on Christmas Eve, we took a train down from the charming ski town of Garmisch, walking through the snow to the big square in Munich, just as the last of the Christmas-tree sellers was heaping his leftovers onto a smoky bonfire.

[229]

We salvaged one small tree and decorated it with cookies and pink piglets in the hotel room. Most of the good Germans were off the snow-padded streets, at home celebrating Christmas Eve with their families or getting ready for late evening church services. But here and there, snug taverns were still open, with stragglers sipping a last stein of cold beer. Germans love—and make—excellent beer and often sell it at open-air stalls, like our hot-dog stands, even in the bitterest cold. Many times I have seen Germans clustered around a sausage stand on a mid-city street, stamping their feet against the cold, enjoying big, spicy, hot sausages, with mustard and a crisp roll. And many times I have joined them.

For German children, the Christmas holiday does not always bring unmixed pleasure. One custom struck me as peculiar: in many families, Christmas gifts are brought by a "Father Christmas" character, usually a relative dressed in St. Nick's costume. Carefully primed beforehand, he scolds the children individually, frightens them with an accurate account of their "bad deeds" of the past year and even carries a switch to add an authentic touch of bad temper and terror to the scene. Often the children are cowed into real unhappiness before Father Christmas turns kind and hands out gifts and sweets. It is a strange custom for a "happy" season, but most Germans seem to feel it does the children no harm.

"Singing clubs" are very popular in Germany and, of course, frequent "meetings" are held during the holiday season. Many of these clubs are simply groups of older men, close friends who like to get together at a neighborhood bar or restaurant with a glass of beer for a few hours of singing.

The effect is usually heart-warming and often melodious. As the night grows longer, the music grows louder—till at last an entire group at a table sits with arms around one another's shoulders, singing and swaying from side to side in rhythm. Frequently, too, a lone customer will join with the accordion player or little band—should there be one— sing a song or two and then be seated, with a happy patter of applause from other diners. Germans put great emphasis on "fellowship" and like these hearty, loud get-togethers. (On the other hand, most Germans are very shy and formal in their relationships until they get to know one another very well. I noticed that at higher schools and universities, most students, even in their teens, address one another as "Mr. Magener" or "Mr. Heinz" and when two students, even two boys, reach the stage of calling each other by first names, the friendship is considered important and very warm.)

About "fun at home": most Germans love big family parties and arrange holiday fun with relation-guests, ranging from grandmothers to babies who may sleep through the activities wrapped in a quilt in a back bedroom. A teen-aged friend of mine told me with sparkling eyes about the great Christmas parties at her house and asked me to come as a guest, the only non-relative of the group, except her boy friend. It was a warm, noisy evening, with waltzing and jitter-bugging going on in the living room, furniture pushed back, till two in the morning. The ceiling was hung with bobbling balloons and crepe paper and the phonograph blared. The whole apartment seemed to sway with noise. And everybody danced with everybody. My teen-aged friend exchanged dances with her grandfather, her cousins and her sister with as much enthusiasm as she whirled around with the handsome young man home from the university for his vacation.

The dining room table was set buffet fashion all night long, with at least half a dozen different cakes and cookies. At midnight, we were served lusty ham sandwiches, hot coffee and sweet liqueurs. Little children stayed awake as long as they could, then curled up in corners to sleep, but the older folk outdanced and outsang the teen-agers until the wee hours.

Also, throughout Germany, at the end of the Christmas-New Year season, a rash of balls, parades and carnival dances breaks out and the often staid Germans go colorfully mad for a few days. In many cities, there are big parades, with bands and *papier-mâché* figures, outsized and grotesque, such as we sometimes have in our Thanksgiving parades. And most of the parties are masquerade affairs that last until dawn. I attended one huge student party in Berlin and it was unrestrainedly wild. Most of the guests were between seventeen and twenty-four—elaborately or very scantily costumed, shouting, laughing and dancing—with liquor a bit stronger than beer being drunk in every corner. Behavior at parties may be controlled and well chaperoned throughout the year, but at holiday time the key word is simply "wild." In fact, during my visit, several German newspapers ran sober editorials, deploring the too-gay balls which are becoming traditional, fearing that this activity may be corrupting to youth. Much as I love gay parties myself, I felt a few chaperones might have calmed this atmosphere. (But then, to the traveler, nothing ever seems exactly as it seems to the people of the country. In Rome, for example, it is a tradition to save old light bulbs during the last months of each year until the moment the New Year rolls in. At exactly midnight, happy Italians tossed light bulbs by the dozen down into the streets of Rome, sometimes from many stories up, till the town echoed and banged like a gang war. And I thought *that* was crazy, too!)

Ireland

What better place in the world to spend St. Patrick's Day than in Dublin? But like so many things in Ireland, this holiday had a touch of sadness in its gaiety: everyone in town turned out for a holiday but the biting weather and too many pinched pocketbooks made it a limited spree.

March 17 last year was a bitter, blowy day and though a few sturdy blossoms still clung to backyard bushes, a light snow covered the ground. In Ireland, St. Patrick's Day is a "holy day of obligation," meaning that Catholics are required to attend Mass, and from seven o'clock till noon, whole families, neat and well-brushed, streamed in and out of the city churches.

The high point of the day, the big St. Patrick's Day parade, turned out to be more like a traffic jam interspersed with marching bands than a real parade. Again, the lack of luxury money was evident: the parade meandered through the city streets of Dublin, made up of a few floats and many, many shiny trucks and wagons representing industries and businesses of the city. If a wealthy merchant had three trucks for his trade, he shined all three, decked them with a bit of green crepe paper and put them in the parade. In one case, a trio of trucks was followed by a proud new cement mixer. But though there was little colorful or paradelike to see, crowds jammed the curb, stamping against the cold, and the lovely gray city of Dublin reverberated with the music of the bands.

For several hours afterward, the in-town streets were jammed with Dubliners celebrating St. Pat's Day with a bit of a promenade before going home for a special midday dinner—whole families walking along, fathers and mothers with several children, all in their dress-up best. As an extra treat, many children were allowed a walk through the old, graceful mid-city park, St. Stephen's Green. Here they tossed hard bread to the flocks of swans which darted through the water, breaking the thin ice with their curved white breasts.

And there was not a single lapel in Dublin without a proud sprig of shamrocks. The shamrocks themselves seemed symbolic of the "bittersweet" mood of the holiday: a true shamrock is a tiny plant, with delicate, three-lobed leaves, no bigger than a child's fingernail—a fragile symbol to represent the pride of a very proud nation.

All the bars are closed on St. Patrick's Day (perhaps one reason why the atmosphere seemed so subdued), so those who could afford it treated themselves to tea and cakes or scones in little restaurants, usually so cold that everyone ate in their topcoats and the windows were blank with steam.

From one o'clock on, a good-sized crowd of Dubliners went to the annual dog show. Ireland, with its eternally green fields, raises some of the finest horses in the world and the little island is also noted for its beautiful dogs. Bench after bench was filled with good-looking animals, ranging

from Irish setters to impeccable, ladylike French poodles.
Going to the dog show is the "chic" thing to do on St. Patrick's Day in Dublin, and the halls were jammed with red-
cheeked citizens in good tweeds and stout walking shoes.
(It is also the only place in Dublin where liquor can be
served on this holiday and the tiny bar was packed with
people only minorly interested in dogs.)

Late that night, we attempted to find a typical St. Pat's
Day dance and, instead of trying an in-town dance hall, we
went to the suburbs. But the dance was as subdued and
un-Irish in feeling as a small country club dance in Nebraska.
I feel sure things were more lively in town. Tickets were
high, about three dollars a couple, and a slow, sweet dance
band played such numbers as *Stardust* and *I Don't Want to
Set the World on Fire.* Most dancers came in couples, dressed
and behaving like American teen-agers out on a semi-formal
date; but some of the casual, happy mood of the dance was
jarred by the great number of "wallflowers," girls in their
middle and late twenties, painfully shy and all dressed up,
sitting on the sidelines, hoping desperately to be asked to
dance. Because women outnumber men on this island and
because social life for teen-agers is so closely restricted, many
girls are just "left out" in life. They remain single, not out
of choice, but because there are not enough men—or enough
men with money for the responsibilities of marriage—to go
around. (I remember a news story on a plowing contest for
women in a country district. The winner was to be awarded
a house and a cash prize—provided she married within the
year. A good farmette, with house and dowry, undoubtedly
met the marriage deadline!)

This particular dance hall was completely without St.

Patrick's Day decorations—no green streamers, no balloons, no paper shamrocks. Among some of the Dubliners I sensed an attitude that such decorations are "corny" and more American than Irish. Every newspaper carried long, detailed stories on the huge St. Patrick's Day parade in New York, reported with interest but with an editorial smile.

"I understand you even paint Fifth Avenue green over in New York for the big day," one man commented. (Actually, the white traffic-divide line *only* is painted green on Fifth Avenue for St. Pat's Day.) The sharp-tongued, sharp-tempered, very proud Irish are wary of what the Irish stand for in the United States—and also just a little jealous. But St. Patrick's Day, like our Fourth of July or Bastille Day in France, is really a holiday in the heart. And I'm sure that Dubliners found more joy in the day than I did.

Good Irish whiskey is one of the outstanding products of this little country and many Irishmen are extremely fond of the native product. The quaint expression "there was drink taken" appears in many newspaper stories explaining traffic accidents or neighborhood brawls.

With this in mind, most parts of Ireland, including Dublin, enforce an old and strange law called the "bona fide" law. In Dublin, for instance, places serving liquor are required to stop serving at ten o'clock sharp and close as soon as the last order is drunk. At about nine forty-five the bartender sings out, "Time, gentlemen." A patron may then hastily order two or three drinks and dawdle over them until about ten-thirty. The law has an unexpected effect: with a time limit in sight, many patrons drink far more than they would if they could order until a later hour.

Also, under the "bona fide" law, any bona fide (or *true*) traveler moving from town to town must be served at any bar or inn outside the city limits. Therefore, when bartenders close up shop in town, a steady stream of cars and bicycles pours out to the suburbs: at the door of each pub or inn, a gentleman asks every caller, "Are you a bona fide?" Invariably, the person answers something such as, "I'm on my way to Galway," and goes in for a drink. The same people may live right in the neighborhood and be "on the way to Galway" five nights a week, but the strange law is still put into practice. Many Irishmen are rather ashamed of the dishonesty, but the law persists.

Holland

A glimpse of a country is better than no look at all. And it took only a short visit to Holland to convince me it was a country I would like some time to see in detail, from the lowlands and windmills right to the concentrated sophistication of Amsterdam. One of the marvels of Europe to a new traveler is the fact that neighbor countries are "just next door," so one afternoon we left Belgium for a drive into Holland, a tiny, orderly country, somehow more lovable because of its sturdiness and monotonous landscape. The fields were fenced off squarely and the brick houses faced the roadside like honorable citizens, each window stretched tight with thick lace curtains.

We reached the town of Maastricht just as the townfolk were breaking up the morning for lunch and in the thin,

[237]

gray winter rain, the streets became a whir of bicycles. It was like getting caught in a panic of dragonflies. This was the Christmas season and every downtown lamppost was hung with mock Christmas gifts, gaily wrapped and bowed in metallic colored paper, swinging and bouncing in the wind, while the streets were arched with colored lights. In food store windows, the well-known balls of red-wrapped boula cheese and great wheels of yellow cheese were stuck with sprigs of holly. The atmosphere of the town was wonderfully prosperous, comfortable—and busy. The Dutch are notable for many things, including cleanliness and industry. Everyone looked sturdily dressed, wide-awake *and* hard at work. Hollanders are also famous for their big appetites, so we put a Dutch lunch to the test.

Our stop was at the Hotel Monopole and we were placed at a table near the window. It was cold inside and out, and a series of chilled Hollanders popped through the door all during lunch for a quick schnapps at the bar before their bicycle rides in the rain. The waiter served lunch with the sleeves of his rough brown sweater showing beneath his white cuffs. However, the steam from the rich, heavy food soon warmed the room.

The menu began with individual servings of tuna fish, hard-boiled eggs and sliced pimiento on lettuce, with home-made mayonnaise; next came a tureen of thick creamed asparagus soup, then platters of fried rumpsteak, served in its own hot grease gravy, a bowl of hot canned peas, dabbed with butter, and a second soup tureen filled with French fried potatoes. Since the table was so crowded, salad made a separate course—quartered tomatoes, hard-boiled eggs, lettuce and a second jug of mayonnaise. Dessert was a bowl of fresh fruit and a platter of little cakes, swirled with whipped cream and daubed with butter icing, with coffee served hot and black. We left the Monopole feeling stout as windmills but curiously touched by the Dutch ampleness and generosity. It was like visiting an old aunt who has prepared all week, feeling the least she can offer young folks these days is a good, home-cooked meal.

After a brief drive, we stopped for a passport check and went into Germany. Another brief drive, another passport check and we were back in Belgium. So close, and yet Germany was the fighting enemy of both little countries in two World Wars. I was able to imagine some of the horror of those days: war against a neighbor near enough to share lunch with.

MAUREEN DALY

was born in County Tyrone, Northern Ireland, and grew up in Fond du Lac, Wisconsin. She first won literary distinction when she was fifteen, with a short story entitled *Fifteen*, which placed fourth in a national short story contest sponsored by *Scholastic* Magazine. The next year she won first place with a story called *Sixteen*, which was selected for the annual O. Henry Memorial Award volume. Her first novel, *Seventeenth Summer*, won the Dodd, Mead Intercollegiate Literary Fellowship contest and quickly became a best seller. She has never stopped writing since—writing vigorously, simply and always with a new appeal.

Her articles and short stories have appeared in many national magazines; and, as a reporter-columnist for the *Chicago Tribune* and later as Associate Editor of *Ladies' Home Journal*, Miss Daly toured the forty-eight states, talking with and writing about teen-agers, their interests and problems. Her first-hand observations and understanding advice are presented in *What's Your P.Q.* and *Smarter and Smoother*.

Her *Twelve Around the World* is the round-the-globe story of young people abroad, from Nigeria to Iceland, written with the same accuracy, humor and understanding that have made Maureen Daly a round-the-world reading favorite. Two years and thousands of miles of travel went into this book. It has the freshness of a newspaper report, the drama of a novel and the warm appeal in any true story about people.